How to Refocus Your Life

See Beyond the Urgent to the Big Picture –
Through Personal Retreats

Also by Chris Warnky

The Heart of a Ninja: Stretch Your Boundaries

What Just Happened?: The Line

What Just Happened?: The Run

The Heart of a Ninja for Kids

Twelve Traits of a Ninja

Four Traits of a Ninja

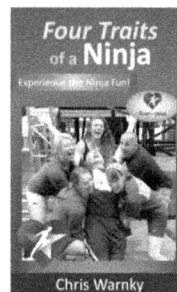

Search Chris Warnky on Amazon.com

How to Refocus Your Life

See Beyond the Urgent to the Big Picture –
Through Personal Retreats

Chris Warnky

Well Done Life LLC

Columbus, Ohio

2021

CHRIS WARNKY

Well Done
Life

Chris Warnky/Well Done Life LLC
1440 Mentor Drive
Westerville, Ohio 43081

Editor: Gwen Hoffnagle
Book Layout © 2021 BookDesignTemplates.com

Ordering Information:
Quantity sales: Special discounts are available on quantity purchases by corporations, associations, and others. For details contact "Special Sales" at the above address.

How to Refocus Your Life: See Beyond the Urgent to the Big Picture –
Through Personal Retreats/Chris Warnky – 1st ed.
ISBN 978-0-9993331-8-1

Dedication

How to Refocus Your Life is dedicated to those looking for a clear-er sense of how well they're living. It's for people who would like to grow by being more intentional in order to get the most out of life. And it's for those who would like to be excellent stewards of what they've been given and to leave a powerful legacy.

Contents

Introduction

The Main Point of *Refocus*

I want to empower you. I believe it's critical to schedule time to think and to refocus your life in order to live a great *intentional* life (I'll get to what I mean by this soon). It's easier to focus when you have an outlined structure to direct you. In *How to Refocus Your Life* (*Refocus*) I provide several options that I have both discovered and created over the years to help you maximize the time you spend assessing your life.

Living Fulfilled

I'm a 64-year-young active Ohioan, enjoying my eighth year of retirement from corporate leadership, living, writing, and playing fully. For years I was consumed by the demands of the moment that continually came my way and the pressures of "You must do this now! It's urgent! It has to get done!" I'm still sometimes overwhelmed by such demands. Living with a sense of urgency is a challenging and depressing way to live. This mentality takes much of the enjoyment, peace, and feeling of fulfillment out of my life.

Over 20 years ago I read some books that challenged me to make it a priority to spend quiet time away, by myself, to stop and think about me and my life. Through these suggestions and my personal experiences I discovered that by taking time to stop, get context, and think holistically, I've been able to live with much more perspective, creativity, enjoyment, peace, confidence, and fulfillment, and have gotten better results from the activities that are most important to me.

You Should Write a Book

Over 10 years ago I had just returned from one of my personal retreats, what I now call *Refocus Sessions*. My co-worker, Trey, was aware that I was investing time this way approximately every two months. In a short conversation across the aisle between our cubicles, he said he was intrigued. He wanted to know what I did and how I did it.

After I shared some of my process and experiences with Trey, he encouraged me, "You should write a book about your personal retreats." This was the first time someone encouraged me to write a book about how I live my life, and his comment remained in my mind. I've become an author of several books about my ninja warrior experiences, and I always had in the back of my mind that someday I was going to write that *Refocus* book that Trey requested. It didn't leave me. It's amazing the impact a short statement can have.

Trey and I aren't still in contact, but I hope someday we get to reconnect so that I can thank him and share with him the impact he has had on both me and the lives of *Refocus* readers. Thanks for the challenge, Trey.

I'm excited to tell you about the processes and tools I've developed over the past 50 years that have helped me and which I believe can help you, too.

Reading *Refocus*, I hope, will convince you of the power of taking the time to stop and gain true life context. My processes and tools should provide the structure you need to make this a valuable investment for you. Taking a break from your busy life to intentionally pause for reflection might feel counterintuitive, but it can actually make you more efficient and more fulfilled.

The Structure of *Refocus*

The first portion of *Refocus* is about why Refocus Sessions are so important. Next I share how I was drawn to investing time in this way and my experiences during my Refocus Sessions, and then you'll read about what I believe to be the value of structure, for just about anything, and especially for personal retreats. Following that I provide three levels or versions of Refocus Sessions. I start with the simple and expand to two deeper levels of thinking and structure. Hopefully one of these levels works well for you.

The next segment of *Refocus* includes a list of creative things you can add to your experience, tips on how to apply what you learn from your Refocus Sessions to your daily life, and examples of the results I've experienced and things I've changed for the better in my life.

The balance of the book describes additional refocusing tools I've developed and used over the years that help me understand where I am and how I want to improve. These include a quick snapshot of your life, a daily journaling routine, a Life Assessment Wheel, a way to assess how you're using your time relative to your natural passions and skills, and a way to assess how you create and use your energy.

Refocus is packed with options and tips to help you assess your life and gain clarity about where you are, where you would like to go, and how you can get there. Pick and choose the sections that resonate most with you.

I hope you find all the parts of *How to Refocus Your Life* stimulating and helpful. Enjoy!

Your Goals for Reading *Refocus*

What would you like from *Refocus*? Taking the time now to clearly record what you want from this book will provide you with more focus for your reading and study. Write it down on a blank page in *Refocus* or on a separate piece of paper, or record it in your favorite electronic device. Defining your intent will help your mind seek the golden nuggets that will be most helpful for you. It will provide a greater return on your investment.

Chapter 1

Gaining Context

My Finger

I was lying on the couch next to my wife, Carolyn, at my son's home in the Cleveland area. We were enjoying some conversation with Tim, my son, and Bonnie, his wife, while their kids were falling asleep in their bedrooms. I decided to try one of the occupational therapy exercises I had used while rehabilitating from a concussion a few months earlier, in which I would jump from focusing on an object at one distance to another object at another distance. I had found it to be a useful exercise for training my eyes to work in tandem.

I put my hand out in front of me with my finger sticking upward. I looked beyond my finger and could clearly see the TV and the kitchen in the background. Then, as in the exercise, I jumped both my eyes to focus on my finger, which was only 12 inches away from my face. When I do this, my eyes are immediately drawn to my finger, and it comes quickly into the best focus my eyes can provide. The background beyond my finger becomes blurry – not as clear and sharp. I can intentionally focus beyond my finger, taking it out of focus and seeing sharply the landscape beyond, but I'm not able to focus on both the finger right in front of me and the landscape beyond it. I have to choose, and my eyes are naturally drawn to what is directly in front of me.

I believe this is the way we live our lives. We're quickly drawn to the objects and activities that are right in front of us, causing the bigger picture to become less clear. The background becomes clear again when we take the time to slow down, observe, and think. When we focus on the larger landscape, we squint less, feel less tension, enjoy a greater depth of field, and see so much more than just the detail of whatever is directly in front of us demanding our attention.

It's easy to fall into a pattern of looking only at what's directly in front of you. It's like having a microscope strapped to your head aligned with your eyes. You see the minute detail, and less of what is going on around you.

I believe we must nurture both perspectives in order to have a fulfilling life, and it requires intention to see the big picture while we live our lives in the detail directly in front of us. You might have heard the analogy of the corporate employee working hard to climb the company ladder. They make excellent progress, only to find out in the end that the ladder is leaning against the wrong building – not the one they believe is most important.

Another good analogy is focusing on "doing things right" instead of ensuring you are first "doing the right things." Doing things well is a worthy goal, but if you invest time in doing less important things very well, it hinders your ability to get the most important things done. You should first evaluate what is most important, then do those things particularly well. How do you relate to this analogy?

Does it provide you with a context for living your daily life more ef-
fectively?

Context First

Context provides framework and perspective. For example, I feel
strongly that I should provide context for my answer to a question.
The context can make all the difference in how my answer is under-
stood, especially when it includes assumptions that are different
from those of the person I'm talking to. I often provide context before proceeding to the answer to a question, and am often
interrupted with responses to the background information I'm
providing. I don't ever get to my answer because the other person
hasn't listened all the way through my extended comments. Barriers
to communication ensue. My natural orientation works well with
people who listen well, but though it feels counterintuitive, I have to
recognize when it's prudent to provide my answer first, then provide
the context if needed.

Clouds

I was at a park during a Refocus Session, and I looked up and saw
the clouds in the sky. During my first quick glance I didn't see any
movement. It seemed the clouds were standing still in the sky. When
I stopped and stared at the clouds, I gained true context about what
was really happening. By stopping, being still, and watching for an
extended period, I saw the movement of the clouds in relation to sur-

rounding trees and structures. Something was moving. It was either me, or the clouds, or both.

When we take the time to stop and observe, we see what is really happening. The clouds were moving while I was standing still on the ground. Technically the Earth was also moving, but we don't ever see or feel that.

We and our environment are constantly moving and changing. It's easy to miss what's really happening in our lives when we don't stop to truly observe our situation. Are we living with intention, or are we just going wherever the wind happens to be blowing? Taking the time to stop and observe is what gives us *context* about what's really happening.

Head Spinning?

Do you ever feel like your head is spinning out of control in response to all the activity going on around you? Many of us live this way. It makes it difficult to move forward. Just as with your physical body, when your mind spins around and around it's difficult to move confidently forward. You feel pulled in many directions at the same time and aren't sure where you'll end up.

The processes and tools I share later in the book get to the heart of the problem you might be facing. Too much is going on, and too quickly. You are continually bombarded with information that can overload your senses and thinking. Like Will Rogers said, "When you find yourself in a hole, stop digging." I believe the solution to much of this challenge is to stop, take a breath, observe your surroundings, think intentionally about where you are and what is going on, and then about how to identify and address the things that are most important to you.

Fog

A few years ago I was driving home from a Christmas Eve celebration at an in-law's house. It was night and a snowstorm was upon us. It was only about a 20-minute drive back to Tim's house where we would be staying for the night, but those were some of the longest minutes of my life as I did everything I could to see and stay on the narrow, winding, two-lane roads. The snow was thick and coming down hard, right into my windshield, as the strong winds were blowing it directly at us. It was nearly impossible to see ahead. I was extremely tense, hoping I wouldn't drive off the road that was caked with white. It was a scary experience. I was so thankful it was finally over after 35 minutes of tense driving.

Have you ever had to drive in a snowstorm or heavy fog? You become much more cautious. You squint to see in front of you, your grip on the steering wheel gets very tight, and you lean forward toward the windshield to try and see the best you can. You drive a lot more slowly, trying to be sure you're staying within the lines on the road, constantly checking the rear-view and side mirrors hoping no one will run into you because of how hard it is to see.

In contrast, on a beautiful clear day you lean back in your seat, one hand resting gently on the steering wheel – maybe two if you're a more cautious person. The view of the road is wide and clear and you're relaxed, knowing that it's easy to stay within the lines of the road. Your trip is easy, enjoyable, and if there are no mishaps you reach your destination in good time.

It's easy in life to slip into a snowstorm or fog through which you can't see much of what is in front of you – in which you have a hazy view of life. Not much is sharp or clear. You can feel like you're simply going through the motions.

Rushing wildly and aimlessly through life can feel like being caught in a dense fog or snowstorm. You're moving, but you aren't sure where and what else might be in front of you that you'll have to negotiate. You might also feel numb as you get caught up in the status quo of life, where life becomes muted and dull, and where you feel drained of energy.

Taking the time to stop, observe your surroundings, and think clearly can take you out of this terrible fog. It's amazing the value you can gain from intentionally stopping to refocus on what is going on around you.

The Long-Term Perspective

I've heard it said that those who experience life with an hour-by-hour mindset are employed by those who live day by day, who work for those who live week by week, who work for those who live month by month, and so on. The person with the broadest perspective, be it of time or space, lives with parameters and expectations much different from those of someone with a narrow perspective. They see so much more.

Facebook creator Marc Zuckerberg is said to think in terms of century to century. I'm happy when I'm focusing out a year or a little

more. I believe this gives me a healthy perspective and a big advantage over those who aren't willing to invest the time to think this
big.

Highly Valued Thinking Time

I highly value quality thinking time away, and I'm not alone. Others have stated the value of taking time to get away and think:

> *Without great solitude no serious work is possible.*
> —*Pablo Picasso*

> *Jesus, Buddha, Confucius, Mohammed, Gandhi – every outstand-
> ing religious leader in history spent much time in solitude, away from
> the distractions of life.*
> —*David J. Schwartz,* The Magic of Thinking Big

Human Becomings

I love the observation that I first heard from author and speaker
Matthew Kelly. He shared that though we're known as "human be-
ings," in our actions and in how we speak it often seems we're more
like "human doings." Our focus seems to be more on what we are
doing or have done – our accomplishments – rather than who we are
and what we have become.

I really like his view of us as "human becomings." We don't stay
the same. We either get better or worse. The way we think and the
things we do or don't do create what we're becoming. It's so power-

ful to think in this way and it leads me to want to live so much more intentionally, seeing the big picture so that who I'm becoming is the person I want to be, not the opposite. This is what I mean by living an *intentional* life.

Who are you becoming based on the way you're currently living? I hope it's the person you want to be becoming, and I hope after our time together in *Refocus* that you'll be even more *intentional* and fulfilled in the process.

Chapter 2

How About You?

How Well Are You Living Your Life?

How do you feel you're doing right now? How well are you living your life? What criteria do you use, or could you use, to make that determination? The criteria you use, or don't use, makes a tremendous impact on how you answer these questions.

If you've taken the time to ask yourself these questions, how often do you do it and how do you conduct this critical life evaluation? These are important questions if you want to be more intentional about your life.

How do you stop and think clearly about the big picture of your life? If you have a regular practice, how well is it working for you? How can you improve it? How can your practice have greater impact on what you're becoming? There are many ways you can approach big-picture questions. Some are much more effective than others. Evaluating how you execute this process can significantly increase the value of your time investment.

I believe these are powerful questions that can help guide and inform your life and lead you to a better place. To achieve the results you desire, you must live intentionally. You can do this by investing the time in yourself to stop, observe, and think about where you are and where you would like to go.

Your Future

What will or could your future look like? How do you know? What signs provide insight into what it will be? What if you could change or direct your future? You can! You can decide today what you would like your future to look like and you can set into motion a plan and take steps to move toward that future. I can't guarantee that you will achieve your exact perfect future, but I'm fully convinced you can move in that direction and potentially realize much, if not all of it, if you do it with intention.

Some people take each day as it comes. Others dream of a life they would like to have or an impact they would like to make, then develop a plan and action steps to move them forward in that direction.

I want to be one who is intentional and moves forward toward a purpose, to leverage who I am and what I have, and to be a good steward of what I've been given. I hope you feel the same way.

Where Is Your Focus?

When you think in terms of your priorities, are you more focused on doing things right, or on doing the right things? It's important to do both, but I believe the order is critical. To live your best life, you should first determine the right things to do and then focus on doing them right or well.

How confident are you that you're doing the right things? By the end of *Refocus* you'll be confident that you're doing the right things, or at least have a road map for how to go about doing the right things, and you will have developed a plan to do more of those right things well, if you so desire.

Chapter 3

Clarity Is Important

Good Stewardship

I was raised to believe that I was given many talents and skills. I believe I'm called to be a good steward of what I've been given in order to honor God. I want to be in the position to hear Him say daily, "Well done, good and faithful servant."

How do I know how I'm doing? What criteria should I use? How can I be confident that I'm being a good steward? Over the years I developed a number of standards or baseline beliefs about myself and who and what I've been called to be and do. In these next pages I share several of them. These provide the criteria with which I assess my life. If you haven't taken the time to develop such standards for yourself, I encourage you to do so. When you're clear about who you are and what you want, it's easier to assess where you are and what you need to do to reinforce that or change in order to make intentional forward progress.

Mission, Vision, and Goals

Many years ago, after I read a stimulating book, I decided I wanted to be clearer and more intentional about my life. One of the ways to do this was to take the time to establish a clear mission and vision for my life; something that clearly defined me, who I was, and where I wanted to go.

Each year, and often each month, week, and day, I create goals based on my mission and vision. These goals have brought so much focus and value to my life. It truly feels good to be going somewhere, intentionally.

My Mission

- I reveal God's grace and help people into strong relationships with Him and each other, as I demonstrate and challenge others to live lives of excellent stewardship.
- I provide insight, forums, and tools to better enable others to develop relationships with God and live lives of excellent stewardship with their God-given assets.
- I love and honor my creator God with all my heart, soul, mind, and body. I'm a great steward of everything I have been given. I model and encourage others to do the same. I do this through example by sharing my beliefs, concepts, and ideas, both verbally and in writing; taking action; and providing supportive group environments.

I want all of my thoughts, words, and actions to align with my mission. Through taking the time to think this through and write it down I've become much clearer about who I want to become: more focused, and much more intentional about how I live my life. I've made thousands of little daily decisions that established the life I have today.

Then I took the time to think through and write down my vision for my future. What did I want my life to look like and how did I want to be living?

My Vision

I ensure that Carolyn knows she is number one in my life, and then I do the things that can help make more than 10,000 people stronger in hope and life-stewardship, including:

- Increase their spiritual knowledge and improve their relationship and walk with God
- Remain true to who God created them to be; be more and more consistently engaged in activities that align with their heart, passion, and talent; develop and consistently use their strengths
- Communicate better in relationships
- Think in advance about their plans and actions
- Live with intent
- Make better daily decisions
- Be more fiscally responsible

This was and is my vision of who I would like to be and what I want to be doing. These statements have also kept me focused.

I selected 10,000 as the number of people I would like to positively influence, feeling that it was a very large number. When I first defined my vision I believed I had already positively influenced about 200 people through family, friends, and work. I considered 5,000 as my goal, but wanted to push myself to think even bigger, so I wrote 10,000.

It was hard for me to put this in writing. Did I really want to work at doing the things that would positively impact 10,000 or more people? I wasn't sure, but I was willing to give it a try. I wasn't willing to write 50,000, 100,000, or a million people. Some of the authors I was reading at the time encouraged me to go much bigger, but this was a good stretch for me. Knowing that my target was 10,000 is one of the things that pushed me to become an author. I felt that to reach 10,000 people I would have to reach people I might never meet. Writing a book was one way to do this.

Today I have over 5,000 Facebook friends and another 1,000 followers on Instagram. (Some of my Instagram followers are the same people who are friends on Facebook, but I know some of them aren't). So when I share notes of encouragement or challenge, maybe I'm already partially impacting over half of my vision number. I have also reached hundreds of people through my published books. And I have several additional books in the works.

Maybe someday I will need to raise my target number, but 10,000 has been a great guide for me over the past 20 years or so. The truth is, I may never know exactly how many people I have positively impacted. Regardless, I continue my quest to make a positive difference in as many people's lives as I can, either directly, or indirectly through the ripple effect.

To put something in writing takes guts, and that comes only after you've taken the time to think it through. My vision statement has definitely influenced my behavior. I've been more intentional. I've used these criteria when conducting Refocus Sessions. Having the criteria is so helpful in assessing how well I'm living and directing my life versus just letting it happen.

Goals

For years I've been convinced of the power of goals. I have personally seen how having a goal, and writing it down, changes my life. It provides the focus and intention I need to get things done.

Early in our marriage Carolyn and I would joke with each other, "Don't write it down or it will happen." We laughed because when we wrote something down it always seemed to eventually come to pass. It was amazing to see how this little action worked. It could be in regard to experiencing something together, like going to Europe; or purchasing something, like a new couch; or replacing our old kitchen knife set – you name it. We would talk about things we might want to have or wanted to do, but once one of us wrote it down on a piece of paper, and especially if the other one knew that it was written down, it seemed to eventually happen, and often quickly.

I have established goals throughout most of our married life, setting annual goals most years, sometimes quarterly and monthly goals, and often weekly goals. Daily goals have always been a core part of my life. What do I want to accomplish today? I love that feeling of getting to check off a goal. It feels so good deep in my core. Goals have also been helpful when I conduct Refocus Sessions. They give me a yardstick with which to measure how I'm doing on my mission.

Goalies

A couple of years ago I was looking for a way to increase my accountability to my annual goals. For many years I had set goals but seldom shared them with anyone. I became convinced of the power of accountability, so I decided to see if I could meet someone who also believed in goals with whom I could be accountable. I was happy and excited about providing someone with accountability while they simultaneously helped me be accountable to my goals.

I thought through my current relationships but I couldn't identify anyone who fit that description. As I was grasping for options, the idea came to mind that I could post a message on Facebook to my 5,000 friends and see if anyone would be interested in joining me in an accountability effort like this. I was surprised when over 20 individuals reached out to be a part of this new group that I was calling "Goalies."

I'm now in my second year of hosting a private Facebook Goalies group. We have agreed to share our personal goals with the group and we report monthly on our progress. The group is for encouragement, support, and accountability. It helps ensure I'm clear on my goals and provides opportunities for reviewing, assessing, and reporting on my progress. It's so much better to do anything as part of a team.

Governing Values

Years ago I discovered how valuable it can be to establish *governing values* for my life — the values I want to live by. They provide another intentional yardstick with which to measure myself. I'm able to assess whether I'm being a good or a poor steward of the life I've been given.

Below are my governing values that I have identified over the past 30 years. I continue to regularly review them, first validating that I'm still committed to each of them, and then assessing how well I'm living each of them.

- Out of gratitude for His love and grace to me, I love God with all my heart and I reflect to others that my base and drive come from Him.
- I consistently live a holy life of integrity before God and man.
- I am committed to and love Carolyn, supporting her in as many ways as possible.
- I encourage and set an example for Carolyn and our kids to live lives of grace and integrity.
- I live a life of consistent balance.
- I remain physically fit, staying physically active on most days (targeting no more than 170 pounds).
- I am always making positive impacts on people's lives, especially through relationships.
- I consistently invest in thinking time – reflectively, creatively, and for the future.
- I invest in planning and preparation to generate better end results.
- I make wise financial investments that support my spiritual and physical needs and those of others.
- I maximize my abilities and capacity and those of others, especially through my coaching and through recognizing and expressing appreciation for others' actions.
- I have fun and enjoy most everything I do.
- Through all of my experiences I constantly grow in depth and width of knowledge and wisdom.

You might rank some of these values higher on your list, and you might not even consider some of my values to be yours.

Life Priorities

During the past several years I have prioritized six themes to help me make decisions about how to use my time. I strive to incorporate these into any activity I do or commit to doing. I feel most happy about my time-investment when all of these are experienced within the same event. The six are:

- Worship of God
- Enjoyment
- Relationships
- Experiences
- Learning and Growth
- Contribution

My Last Letter

A few years ago, sitting in a chair under a tree in our front yard on a sunny afternoon, I came across an interesting article in an AARP magazine. It was encouraging readers to write a "last letter" to family and friends, and to do it now. This is a letter that you would like your spouse and/or loved ones to receive after you've died. The article talked about the value of this exercise to the writer and especially to the recipients. The concept was extremely intriguing. I began to imagine the power that a letter like that could have for my friends and family after I'm gone, especially if I were to be taken suddenly from this planet with no time to make final statements to those I love. I decided I was going to give it a try. It was a powerful and context-providing experience that I highly recommend.

Through creating a last letter I was able to ensure that I have truly said all I want to say to the people I love. Some people never get that chance, as death comes quickly and unexpectedly. This was a way to ensure that that wouldn't happen for me or my loved ones.

It was a powerful exercise to write a letter in an "after I'm gone" mindset. It really made me think about what it will be like for them when I'm gone. It forced me to think clearly about what I would want them to know when I'm no longer able to speak. I addressed my appreciation and my wishes for them when I'm no longer here.

I'm sorry not to be sharing this letter with you – it's way too personal and emotional; but I encourage you to challenge yourself with the powerful experience of writing your own last letter.

My Eulogy

My father-in-law died unexpectedly in 2001 while he was in his early seventies – too young, from my perspective. His early death had a number of significant impacts on me. I participated with Carolyn and her mom as we went through the funeral arrangements. A lot of hard decisions needed to be made. We continually tried to define what we thought he would have wanted for the ceremony. It was a taxing experience, and even then we didn't know for sure that the choices we made were what he would have wanted.

Coming out of that experience I decided to define each of the key things I would want for my funeral. These are now documented on a piece of paper folded into the pages at the beginning of my favorite Bible chapter, Psalm 139, in my study bible. That is where Carolyn will find it when I'm gone.

I also decided to define what I wanted, or hoped, people would say about me at my funeral. Doing this gave me a goal, a lifestyle, a reputation to seek as I manage my day-to-day thoughts, words, and actions. If I do the right things, people will say the things I would like them to say about me. They will simply be sharing about the way I lived.

This has been a powerful life-guiding document:

Carolyn

- He loved me very much.
- He prioritized listening and understanding me.
- He provided very well for our entire family.
- He took care of himself: spiritually, physically, and mentally.
- He loved God.
- He was a good guy, real, transparent, and always planning, even his funeral. :-)
- He worked hard, had a strong commitment to stewardship, and loved me and his kids.
- Starting at around age 45, he was always reading, learning, and starting something new to personally grow or to touch others' lives and hopefully help make them better.
- He loved team-based sports.

My Kids

- He had a spiritual core that affected everything he did.
- He loved Mom a lot, which was a great model for us.
- He loved us and provided well for us and was more interested in our character than anything else.
- He always cheered us on.
- He was fun, a joker, and energetic.
- He loved team sports.

A friend

- He challenged me and wanted me to think more and be a better steward.
- He served continually, and frequently shared his experiences and learning.
- He was very open about his life.
- He encouraged and supported me without judgment.

Someone I served

He was very dedicated, consistent, and committed.

Chapter 4

Our Powerful Minds

The way God designed our minds is amazing. They're so powerful. Our minds control and direct our lives. Our thoughts and beliefs lead to our feelings and actions, which create our futures. Understanding and controlling our minds is decisive in determining the way we live. I wonder if we take our minds as seriously as we should relative to their impacts on our lives.

Buy the Thinking

Early in my coaching career I worked with a client on a pro bono basis. I was still working in my corporate job as a project manager and I didn't want to have to deal with formal corporate approval for having a second job. I was a relatively new coach and I wanted to help people and practice my new skill.

We met biweekly for seven sessions. Our sessions were excellent, but my client seldom followed through on his commitments from our prior sessions. Although I was disappointed in him, as his coach I knew that ultimately the follow-through was about him, and didn't take it personally. Even though his follow-through was pretty close to nothing, a good session for him meant focusing on what he had learned from his actions on his commitments.

At the end of our seventh session I informed him that I was going to be retiring from my corporate job and I would begin charging for my coaching services. I sent him a copy of my rate sheet so he could see what the investment would be for each of the three packages I provided. They were five, ten, and fifteen-session bundles, providing more savings the more sessions the client purchased. I don't share confidential information with Carolyn, but I told her I had a client who seldom followed through on his commitments and who likely wouldn't be hiring me going forward. He didn't appear to be using our sessions to improve his life.

As I closed our final pro bono session, I asked the typical open-ended question that salespeople ask: "Where would you like to go from here? You've seen my rate sheet." I knew in my heart there was no way he would move forward with me, but to my surprise he said he wanted to buy a year of sessions! "Can you pull something to-gether for me to be able to do that?" I told him I could while I tried to hide my shock. I probed gently and a little deeper. I asked, "What's leading you to want to buy a full year?" I didn't want to talk him out of it, but I wanted to better understand what was behind his request. He responded, "I know I've not been very good at doing what I keep saying I will do, but I want to buy the thinking that I'm starting to de-velop as I work with you. My first thirty years of thinking have led me to where I am today. I know it will take more time to significantly im-prove the way I think. I want to buy the thinking, which I'm confident will spill into improved actions. I love this new powerful way of think-ing."

I developed a full-year package for him, 24 biweekly sessions, and he purchased them. We continued to meet and, as he predicted, he began to make significant changes in the way he thought and in his actions. At nine months he asked to add another six months of coaching to the end of his package. This was a beneficial support system for him, and he was significantly changing who he was – in a good way.

His thinking led to his actions, as it seems to do for all of us. This is one of the reasons I was called to write *Refocus*. If you follow the steps outlined, I'm confident it will improve your life. It has for me.

Imagination

The Noise Downstairs

When you hear a noise downstairs in the middle of the night, you might envision someone breaking into your house and running into something as they approach the stairs to come attack you. You immediately go through the experience of being attacked. Fear kicks in and you imagine even more details about what could or will happen. They might have a gun. There might be more than one of them. They're looking for an upstairs room to find a stash of money. Your anxiety skyrockets, and you might tremble and sweat from the experience. Your breathing becomes shallow. You try not to move, concentrating on hearing the next sound. The silence can be even scarier.

It could have been the air conditioner blowing a piece of paper into a pencil, which rolled off the table onto the floor. It doesn't matter what really happened; what matters is what you saw happening in your mind. That is what you live.

Many live in constant fear due to a mindset that creates visions like this over and over. We live through the experiences we see in our minds, both to our benefit and to our detriment.

When we vividly imagine something, we also experience the emotion tied to it: joy, fear, peace, a sensation – you name it. We experience what we imagine, whether it's real or not. We feel that emotion and experience it in our physiology.

Imagine seeing your favorite movie star or shaking hands with a famous athlete. Chances are your heart would race with excitement. You hope you don't say the wrong thing or come across poorly. You think about how you look and what you're wearing because you want to make a good impression. What you're *thinking* results in a feeling of excitement, confidence, or fear.

A New Skill

As an American Ninja Warrior, I am often confronted with new physical and mental obstacles. When I'm attempting a ninja skill for the first time, like jumping from a trampoline to a bar in front of me, if I see it as too far to reach, it's too far. In my mind I see me missing the bar and falling to the ground, wondering if I'll fall safely or if I'll hurt myself in the process. I shake my hands, trying to convince them I can catch the bar. I keep shaking them because I'm really afraid to try it.

This fear can be paralyzing, holding me back. I step toward the trampoline and look at the bar, and then I step back again, looking at the ground. I turn to glance quickly again at the bar and then I turn away again. I might repeat this process multiple times. My fear of what could happen takes over.

When I see the bar as being a reasonable distance away, or if I've caught the bar at that distance in the past, suddenly I find I can catch it. Repeatedly I've found that in my mind I overestimate the difficulty of something and I shut down due to fear – not of reality but of what I've created in my mind.

It takes baby steps, trying it over and over, to learn how far I can go. I'm often able to go much farther than I originally thought. There have been times when I leapt far enough but didn't catch and hold on to the bar because my mind didn't think I could; I touched the bar and fell to the ground. With a few more attempts my mind learns that I can catch and grab the bar, so I do it, and often with ease. This builds my confidence. The limitation wasn't necessarily my ability, but my mind, which had to align with my ability.

The Recital

I've seen that same limitation lived out in various situations. When I was a child, at a piano recital I was playing the song "As the Caissons Go Rolling Along." About midway through the song my mind froze, and my ability shut down, because I suddenly hit a wrong note. I feared what people were thinking about my ability. In my mind I couldn't play that song any further, even though in my own home or at the piano teacher's house I could play it easily and perfectly. Immediately I stood up from the bench and with my hands over my face walked away from the piano to my seat in the auditorium. I was humiliated and embarrassed to be there. I wanted to be somewhere else, somewhere safe and by myself where people wouldn't judge me. This took place because of one wrong note and a very creative, negative thought in my mind.

Looking back, I'm pretty sure those in the audience hurt with me as I played that one wrong note. They probably hoped I didn't feel too badly about it and they were looking forward to hearing the rest of the song. Most of them probably felt sorry for me as I left the piano bench, knowing that it must have been hard for me to miss that note. I likely had the empathy and support of the full auditorium, parents and friends. But that is not how I interpreted it at the time in my mind. Instead it resulted in an incomplete performance, damaging my confidence for my future.

Spelling

Being outspoken and one of the leaders of the group, I was offered the facilitator and flip-chart-scribe role for a discussion with my peers on the President's Advisory Council of the John Maxwell Team. We were identifying and selecting strategies and options to overcome an issue we were facing. I kindly and politely declined, to generously let someone else take that prominent position in front of the group.

I've not been a strong speller in the past, and have been misspelling words since I was in grade school. It has been a difficult skill to develop as an adult. Because of this, I've felt afraid of misspelling words on a board or flip chart in front of others, telling myself that if I misspelled something, my reputation, value, or worth would be stripped from me by others. I didn't want to be reduced as a person because others could see my limited spelling capability.

When leadership opportunities have surfaced that required writing on a board in front of others, when possible I have slowly moved to a less visible part of the room. I would try to have no eye contact with the person in charge. I would keep my head down. I didn't want to be found. If I were, I knew it would be disastrous, whatever disastrous would be. I didn't need to know details; I knew it would be a terrible experience. Over the years I've missed many opportunities to lead through the stories I created due to this negative thinking.

When I see myself as being unsuccessful, I usually am. When I see myself as having success in those situations, moving forward with confidence, I usually perform well. My actual experience is clearly impacted by how I think about it. How I think about it is even more important than the reality itself.

Our Perspective Changes Everything

Our perspective determines what we believe we can accomplish. It absolutely matters, and yet it's easy to get sucked into the day-to-day minutiae and miss the broader picture. When we live and operate from our percieved limitations, we can get stuck in that narrow perspective. If making it to the next hour or the next day is what we're envisioning, then we'll spend our time on only short-term activities.

Some of us see our life as being like the captain of a little ship out in the middle of the sea with the waves tossing and turning us every possible direction. We're at the whim of the wind and the sea, and we can't see a shoreline or land. We're doing our best to stay afloat, not knowing where we're going or if we'll even survive the long trip.

In contrast, some have the awareness to see and experience things from an airplane pilot's point of view, from far above, looking down at the little boat. The pilot has context, or perspective, and can provide instruction to the boat's captain about how to set the sails, how to use the rudder, and which direction to sail the boat. The pilot can see the nearest land and how much longer a storm will potentially last and in what direction the boat is drifting. With that perspective and information, the captain can be intentional with their actions. This perspective usually comes from experience. I love this analogy for understanding the *intentional* perspective.

I breathe deeply and think clearly when I see things from a pilot's perspective. The simple act of staring at the moon provides a big-picture context for my life here on Earth. I also gain great perspective on even more of my life by conducting Refocus Sessions. The amazing thing is we all have the potential to have this perspective.

The Impact and Power of Awareness

Our perspective is dependent on our awareness – what we see, feel, and know from our experiences. Our awareness defines our perspective of where we are, what's happening around us, and what's likely to be coming. Awareness is so critical. When we aren't aware, life can just happen to us instead of our living intentionally, attuned to our surroundings.

A young child isn't aware of the danger of cars driving on a street, so they believe they can run into the street at any time. Our parents worked hard to educate us about that danger. That awareness is critical to our safety.

Driving

As adults, if we're driving and planning to change lanes, awareness is critical. If a car is passing us on the left and we're distracted or don't take the time to be aware of our surroundings by checking our mirrors and head-checking to our left, the other cars don't seem to exist. We haven't taken the time and effort to be aware of our surroundings. This is also a great analogy about how life works. Seeing the broader picture helps us make wiser choices about how to think and act.

Food

I was a typical American guy, eating whatever I wanted whenever I wanted, until... my doctor told me my cholesterol ratio was not good. My HDL, the good cholesterol, was too low and my LDL, the bad cholesterol, was too high. He asked me to begin taking some medication to improve my condition. One word, *medication*, changed everything for me. I don't like taking medication if I can help it. That word sent me into a major lifestyle change and a whole new awareness about my food.

Our awareness of our food's nutritional value has a tremendous impact on our feelings, choices, and actions. When we aren't aware of the contents of our food, we eat based on taste and the feeling of being full. That can lead to overeating and feeding our bodies unhealthy foods, creating potential problems, sometimes in the short run and always in the long run. If we're focused and make consistent choices based on the number of calories we eat and the nutritional content of our foods, we can live much healthier and longer lives. These choices can create mental battles when we're facing the desire for a certain taste, knowing the calories are more, maybe even much more, than we need.

I'm personally focused on limiting my saturated fat intake due to my past cholesterol levels. This awareness and knowledge has had a gigantic impact on my food choices and how often I choose to eat, and of course on my long-term health.

Health

I was reminded of the power of awareness when I had a prostate biopsy due to an elevated PSA test result. I became a bit anxious as I anticipated the biopsy procedure itself, the recovery period, and the results that would come from it. I had to wait 10 days to hear the results. I handled the waiting period relatively well, but the possibility of having cancer was definitely on my mind.

The results were negative, and I was relieved and thankful, and was reminded of the power of awareness. In some ways nothing had changed, and in some ways everything had changed, even though the facts hadn't changed. Some prostate inflamation existed in my body whether I had known about it or not. Having the awareness of my elevated PSA caused me to take steps to evaluate the situation. I had a more complex blood test and then a biopsy, which, based on the results, could have created even more actions. A new discovery or awareness can change everything through the actions you take to influence your future.

One of the primary focuses of a coach is to help clients become more aware so they can better deal with their situations and goals. It can change everything. I've seen it over and over with my clients. I'm convinced that increasing your awareness is vital to living your best life.

Refocus Sessions

Chapter 5

My Personal Retreats

Deeper Thinking Begins

My early life was all about play, sports, and competition. I didn't like to read; it took me away from playing. My conversations and thinking were about a better way to swing the bat, how to improve my basketball shot, or how to improve my wrist shot in hockey. Most of my time was spent doing – working on improving – and not even talking about it. My best friend, Bob, was a reader, especially of novels and comic books. Not me.

I spent little time thinking about life, me, or my world. I was full of doing and enjoying. I didn't do well in school because I had no interest in reading, thinking, or learning. Other than the required reading, which I did poorly, I didn't read. My lack of desire to learn reduced my ability to retain information, but I didn't see the value in it. Like many kids, I wanted to play, and learning and school kept me from my play time.

A grade of C was just fine with me. That meant that I could move on and continue to play. I learned that if I got a D, a B could offset it. Because of the creative and play aspects of gym, art, and sometimes music, I often earned A's and Bs in those. They helped offset the Ds I occasionally got in English, math, and science. I viewed school as an obstacle, not a tool for my future. This attitude continued through grade school, junior high, high school, and even college. Reading and thinking were not a part of my life.

My process of becoming what I consider a deeper thinker was shaped by some key experiences and exposure to new perspectives. In the process I have gotten to know myself on a deeper level and I'm now aware of how powerful the quality of my thinking is in shaping the quality and outcome of my life.

Early in my working career I took the Myers-Briggs personality test. Such tests are used to assess and predict behavior as well as evaluate character. I learned that my personality was an ENTJ: E for Extrovert, N for Intuitive, T for Thinking, and J for Judging. Although I was slightly extroverted, my ratio was relatively balanced "E" to "I" (Introvert).

As I have aged, I think my "I" has overtaken my "E." I seem to love opportunities to be alone, read, think, and deeply ponder various topics.

Reading

I was lying in the back of our minivan while Carolyn was driving. Our family was driving to Wichita, Kansas, to visit my parents. We were going to be driving all night, rotating drivers, for about 16 hours to get to my parents' house. To ease the monotony of the dark drive I had checked out a couple of books on tape from the library. One or two were fiction and one was a management book called *First, Break All the Rules*, published by Gallup and compiled by Marcus Buckingham and Curt Coffman.

I listened to one of the fiction books for a little while, but I couldn't get into it, so I thought I would try the management book. It lit a fire in me that I had not felt in years. The content and challenges reflected my mindset as a manager. I was pumped and excited. I listened to the whole book during that night and couldn't wait to get to a store to buy a physical copy so I could make notes in it the next time through. Since that day I've not been the same.

It was in the early 2000s that I started to read for growth and development. I was about 45 when I first enjoyed that book that I felt would help make me a better manager at work. From that point I developed a tremendous desire to learn new concepts that could help me grow. I discovered that I often learned these from... books and reading. I was becoming a reader for the first time in my life. I couldn't stop. Books about personal growth challenged me, changed my thinking, and opened a whole new world for me.

I was sitting in the lobby of my office, taking a break and skimming the company news magazine. It had a "Recommended Books" section. A book on the topic of our thinking caught my eye. I decided to buy it and give it a try. It was the first book specifically about thinking that grabbed my attention: *Thinking for a Change* by John C. Maxwell. It challenged me to establish dedicated thinking times. It had excellent points, tips, and suggestions for improving my thinking that really resonated with me. The first book Maxwell wrote is called *Think on These Things* – a short, thought-provoking book that I loved. A book by James Allen, *As a Man Thinketh*, was also tremendously powerful for me. These books significantly changed my life for the good.

Over the years I have heard and read many quotes about the power of our thinking. I believe in the Henry Ford quote, "Thinking is the hardest work there is, which is probably the reason why so few engage in it." With this new and unexpected insight, I wanted to work hard on improving the quality of my thinking. I became convinced that better thinking would absolutely translate to a better life.

Personal Time Away

H. Dale Burke's *Less Is More Leadership* is the book that led me to my first personal retreat. Burke wrote about the value of taking time away to do intentional thinking and reflecting. I decided to give this a try — to take some time away, by myself, to deal with me and to assess how I was doing and where I was going in my life.

I didn't have much in the way of structure, but I started the process of taking personal retreats at local parks and restaurants. I took with me a pad of paper, a stimulating book I was reading, and my Bible, and I began a new journey of taking reading, reflecting, and thinking times that continues to this day.

For my first session I began with some focused thinking about life, me, how I was doing, and where I was going. I quickly fell in love with these times. They provided me with perspective and awareness that I had never had. It was invigorating, as I was taking a new level of control of my thinking and my life. My retreats evolved over the years, and now I refer to them as Refocus Sessions. I am happy to say that these are some of my favorite times in life.

Deep Questions Family

Sitting in my study in early 2020, I came across an email from coach Bob Tiede that included a list of 365 questions you can ask yourself – a year's worth. The questions originally came from authors Marc and Angel Chernoff. I enjoyed skimming through the list and decided to try to find a way to think through the questions. They were thought-provoking and stimulating.

Then, during a Refocus Session, I had the idea of thinking through the questions with others, which could potentially be even more stimulating. On my Instagram and Facebook pages I asked if anyone was interested in joining me in thinking through the list of questions. I received 12 responses, so I created a small Facebook Messenger chat group.

We have been meeting Thursday nights on video calls, thinking through and then sharing our responses to each of the questions. These have been stimulating times for what we call our Deep Questions Family. We address one question a week. As of this writing we are on question 45, so we have quite a few to go. It's a powerful group, as we gain new and different perspectives. Seven of us have participated regularly and have truly become a close family, sharing deeply about our beliefs and lives.

Thinking times are now an absolutely critical part of my life – not like my first 45 years. I'm very thankful for this life-improving change.

Chapter 6

The Benefits

There are numerous benefits of taking the time to get away to think and refocus.

Easier Decisions

Making decisions is much easier if you have defined criteria to help you make them. Taking the time to stop and think allows you to define what's important to you so you can be much clearer about what you want and what it will take to get there. If I want to remain healthy, exercise is one factor that will provide that benefit. Then the decision to exercise, even when I don't want to do so, is a little easier to fight through. Not easy, but easier.

Because of my desire to manage calories and saturated fat, I don't add butter to anything I eat, we buy low-fat ice cream, and use a kitchen scale to limit ourselves to three-ounce servings. Without thinking about these criteria and my desire for a specific result, I wouldn't have made these decisions. I would skip exercising a lot more often than I do, and I would eat as much ice cream as I want to at least every day of the week. Living without intentional limitations would likely have an adverse effect on the quality of my life.

Through thinking and deciding in advance what I want and what criteria will help me get there instead of just letting things happen haphazardly, challenging decisions are now much easier for me to make.

Greater Confidence

My confidence is greater now as well, because I know I have better context and a clearer perspective on the big picture and the long-term results that will come from the actions I decide to take. Refocus Sessions provide me with both more confidence to take action and the peace that comes from making the right decisions, both now and in the future. I know that I'm much less likely to be surprised or blindsided. I've thought through each of my actions much more thoroughly than I would have in the past.

Preparation also garners greater confidence. I find that my thinking times result in much better preparation for everything I do. I'm not reacting, but rather planning for the result I want. The better I prepare and plan, the greater my confidence in performing any task, and it feels good to be ready.

Smaller Course Corrections

Taking time away to think allows me to assess what I've done and how the results have impacted my life. When I notice that something needs to change, I make smaller adjustments, much more often and more quickly than I used to, resulting in fewer big changes. It's like a guided missile that moves forward, continuously receiving feedback and making corrections – frequent small corrections – to help it stay on target, even toward a moving target. Less frequent corrections can result in having to make more dramatic changes or totally missing my target or goal. My Refocus Sessions allow me to identify and focus on feedback from prior results and to make minor corrections before there's a need for big ones. Small mistakes, small regrets. Big mistakes, big regrets.

More Appreciation

I've also become more thankful for and appreciative of what I have. In 2020 I was on a long hike at Sharon Woods Metro Park in my hometown, appreciating the beautiful early November day that was unseasonably warm. I had to get outside and enjoy it. My heart, mind, and body were feeling weighed down by the pressures of life, the mask-wearing and social-distancing directives of the COVID-19 pandemic, and the presidential election. I was feeling cut off, boxed in, and exhausted by all that was going on around me.

Midway through this peaceful nature walk, my thoughts turned to gratitude and appreciation. I've been given so much; there was a lot to be thankful for. I took inventory of my blessings. I was reminded of the freedom I had even to take that walk at that time, on a weekday, because I was retired and had the flexibility to do so. I was grateful for the beautiful, sunny, November day; the colorful trees; the clear, fresh air to breathe; the nice clean clothes I was wearing; my healthy legs that could take me on this hike; the bright sun shining on my back; the fact that I was well fed and that I and most of my family and friends were healthy and hadn't contracted the COVID-19 virus. These few minutes of shifting my focus to my blessings transformed my whole perspective for the better.

By taking time to stop, think, and notice, I'm more aware of people, things, and experiences that I've been blessed with. I don't take as much for granted in contrast to when I'm doing, doing, doing and going, going, going. The blessings are still there whether I notice them or not, so it's a shame when I don't think about and appreciate them. Not everyone has been blessed with what I have. I want to be thankful for all my blessings. Refocusing helps me do this.

Better Learning and Growth

By taking the time to think about my days and my life, each experience becomes valuable, not a "throw-away." I enjoy and learn from each experience rather than repeating the same actions over and over without learning or growing. I learn, modify my actions, and experience better results, which are rewarding and pleasing experiences.

I love what John C. Maxwell says: "A lesson is repeated until it is learned." I've found that to be so true. If I don't learn from an experience, I tend to experience the same result over and over.

In Dale Carnegie's book *How to Win Friends and Influence People,* he wrote that he invested in evaluation time each Sunday night. He reviewed his past week and identified what he learned from the experiences so he could apply what he learned to the coming week. He shared that this one regular practice had a profound impact on his life. I'm not alone in my belief in the value of these isolated thinking and assessment times. They can, and do, change our lives for the better. They sure have improved mine.

More Creativity

When I'm quiet and patient I identify more creative opportunities and solutions than when I rush things. My thinking moves to a whole new level, or even multiple levels, when I take the time to concentrate and work toward the best solutions, with fewer limits. Many of my most creative ideas have come from my quiet thinking times.

Attending to What's Important

When I'm rushed, I'm drawn to what is directly in front of me — the loudest voice in my head. It might be my boss, my wife, the weeds in the yard – you name it. It's not until I slow down, step back, breathe, and think clearly that I'm able to see the full picture and determine what is truly most important. Slowing down and stopping has helped me ensure that the important isn't neglected or missed but gets the proper attention. People have lost health, recovery, relaxation, regeneration, relationships – even their lives – because the things that were most important were not getting the attention they needed; the urgent crowded out the important. It happens so easily… unless we're intentional.

More to Work With

When I take the time to think back and evaluate what I've recently experienced, I'm able to educate myself about those experiences and monitor what's happening around me. I then have more to work with in making plans and decisions. It feels like living with a college degree rather than a high school degree. I have more knowledge to support my life, goals, decisions, and actions, and I have more perspective. It's a tremendous benefit that many don't take advantage of.

And like other forms of education, it builds on itself. Once you know letters, it opens the door to knowing words. When you know words, you have the possibility of reading and writing sentences. When you can read and write sentences, you can read and write paragraphs, and the learning skyrockets as you read and learn from books.

This is so evident in the difference between Carolyn and me. She lives and works with so much more information because she has read over 10 times the number of words and books I've read during my life. She has been an avid reader all her life. She loves to read and can't stop doing it. I've been reading significantly for only 20 years. I credit her reading with the fact that she understands many things much better than I do, and has so much more context to work with in her life.

An investment today, no matter what day it is, is a significant investment in your future. Everything you're doing compounds. The goal is to make sure you're investing in the right places to get the compounding effect you desire. Hopefully more bread for your head, not just your belly, or only your belly.

Thinking and assessment times are powerful in creating better and stronger minds and, in turn, people. When we invest in these times, we have more to work with.

It's Energizing

It feels energizing to be in control and to see growth and forward movement in our lives. I've felt this and so have my coaching clients. When we stop to think clearly we make better, intentional, thought-through decisions and plans. Having a plan helps us feel in control. We have marching orders that we feel good about. We're not victims of or pawns in other people's desires and plans. We're writing our own stories, the way we want them to go.

My intentional plans don't always go exactly the way I want them to, but they *feel* right. I'm in control of my actions versus responding to outside stimuli or external situations. It feels energizing to be in control of my life and actions. I feel like I'm a king or a lion on the top of a hill when I'm being intentional and doing the things I believe are most important. I love this energized feeling and I'm sure you do as well. Refocusing your life provides that energy.

I've come to believe that energy is the most valuable and limited commodity we have. We all have the same amount of time, which is limited; but within that time we also have periods when we're energized, some of us more than others. Those with the most energy are often those with the greatest success and most joy in life. It feels tremendous to be energized and in the flow of your life. I try to prioritize actions that generate more energy. My Refocus Sessions are a valuable resource for creating that energy. (I share more on the topic of energy in chapter 16.)

Chapter 7

My Process

Now let's take a look at my refocus process. I describe the specific process and steps I take to refocus below. As I wrote above, I allocate dedicated time, somewhere away from my familiar surroundings, with a way to capture my thoughts as they come to mind. Writing works best for me, but you might prefer using your electronic device. Find what resonates and feels most natural for you.

Frequency

How often do I get away for a Refocus Session? It depends on my life situation. In the past I tried to get away for a retreat about once a quarter. Now that I'm retired from corporate life I do so every two to three weeks. You might not be able to conduct them this often, but I encourage you to take a couple of hours at least quarterly to think about and assess what's going on in your life. You'll want to disconnect from the bombarding stimulation of everyday life, and enter into quiet stillness. If you can do this monthly or biweekly, that's even better. Do what works for you at this stage of your life, and adjust the frequency as needed as your life changes.

When and Where

Driving

Where can you best refocus your life? Some try to squeeze in some thinking time while driving, which is better than nothing. But it's not the same as quiet, focused retreat time because there are of course things that happen on the road that require your immediate attention and dilute your ability to fully immerse yourself in introspection. It's not impossible to make notes while driving – I confess I've done this – but it's not advisable from a safety perspective and not optimal from a thinking perspective.

Vacations

Vacations can provide some good get-away time, but hopefully much of this time is intended for recovery from your hard work. Hopefully you're able to enjoy some special experiences during these times, being present where you are and with people you love. You can refocus a bit, but again, it's not ideal. *Vacate* when you're on vacation; be somewhere unique and enjoy that special time.

Dedicated Refocus Sessions

I've found that it's best to set aside targeted times for refocusing, designed specifically for that purpose. I also really like to be somewhere different from my ordinary surroundings. I want a different, fresh environment when possible. A park, cabin, retreat center, resort, city bench, and restaurant have worked well. It's best to be somewhere new and different so you aren't sucked into the thoughts that come to mind when you're in a familiar place. New surroundings can enhance your ability to generate a new, fresh, and different per-

spective. It's fun to experiment to see what works best, and the options are limitless: a playground, in the middle of a hiking trail, on a
raft or boat on the water, or maybe sitting on the top of a mountain.
Do what you need to do to gain a new and fresh perspective and
view.

Time Allocation

Having enough time to truly slow down is critical. Even an hour
can be beneficial, but I encourage you to target between three and
eight hours of time to refocus your life. You might hear "eight hours"
and say to yourself, "What in the world would I do during that time?"
Well, fasten your seatbelt; there's plenty that could easily fill eight
hours or even more. Keep reading.

Again, experiment to determine how much time works best for
you. You can make adjustments for future sessions, making them
shorter or longer. I think you'll find it's difficult to gain much serious
value in a 15- or 30-minute session. You'll likely need more time as
you learn to dive deeper into the process.

My deepest-level Refocus Session, using an analogy I write more
about in chapter 9 – going deeper into the ocean of my mind – can
easily take from six to eight hours or more. At times I've broken a
session into two or three two-hour segments – maybe even a couple
of weeks apart. The key is to create the time to think clearly about
you and your life. You will learn what works best for you. Don't skimp
on yourself; invest in yourself.

Disconnect

I encourage you to disconnect from outside communication and social media during your Refocus Sessions. Distractions hinder the retreat process and create interruptions that steal from this time of intentional clarity. By disconnecting from the noise of everyday life, a new and sharp focus can be realized. It takes just one ping, one ring, or one glance at your phone to get distracted from thinking clearly. I work hard to ensure that my phone and computer aren't distractions. This is one of the reasons pen and paper work so well for me for taking notes. I only get distracted if my pen dies and I need to replace it or I run out of space on my page and have to stop long enough to turn to a clean sheet of paper.

Write

The writing part of my sessions is magical and helps crystalize my thoughts. Writing my thoughts down takes them from the dimensions of my mind into a physical presence that provides space between me and the problem or goal that I'm thinking through, and leads me to objectivity. It's out of my head, more factual, more accurate, and closer to reality. It ensures I'm using the best words to define what I want or how to achieve something.

There is magic as I review what I've written. I often see error in my thoughts or words, or that something needs to change to become more accurate or more practical to apply. Writing, or maybe typing for you, is a powerful step of the process. It's like swinging a lasso around all those wild and disjointed thoughts in my head and pulling them into one cohesive thought – a more holistic concept that can be seen and assessed once it's written on the page before me.

My Checklist

Having a framework or structure helps guide the process. It's a way to narrow my thinking on a topic. To be more intentional, I created a checklist to ensure I had all I needed to make my personal retreats powerful experiences. It's extensive because it's designed to apply to retreats when I stay overnight somewhere as well as to shorter ones. I have used it for years, and hope you find it helpful:

Goal:

☐ Be away for at least 18 hours to slow down, clear my mind, think big-picture, reflect, listen, dream, and evaluate; validate my life and current dreams, goals, activities, and challenges; and read – scripture and other books.

Goal Activities:

☐ Be away from routine (home/work/church)
☐ Exposure to nature/context
☐ Unstructured time/no detailed plan
☐ Quiet, solitude, and observing/listening time
☐ Rest
☐ Exercise/hike – walk through nature
☐ Open thinking: big picture and long term
☐ Significant scripture reading and writing
☐ Discovery; explore new place
☐ Stimulating reading time – read personal-growth books
☐ Applying God's word to my activities
☐ Eat different foods and from different places

Do Not:

☐ Focus on details or routine tasks

Prepare:

☐ Start prep and packing seven days ahead of schedule

☐ Reserve a thought-provoking book on tape for the drive

☐ Get clear directions for the site: hotel, parks, road names, mileages, etc.

☐ Book overnight accommodations ahead of time

☐ Set GPS location on phone navigation program

Items Needed

☐ Refocus Session file

☐ Bible

☐ Thought-provoking books

☐ Possibly one new book to read

☐ *Less Is More Leadership* book

☐ Thinking ideas file

☐ Thinking questions

☐ Retirement notes file

☐ Life management plan

☐ Goals list

☐ Dreams list

☐ Easy Love Matrix (see chapter 15)

☐ Plenty of blank paper

☐ Pens and pencils

☐ iPad e-reader

☐ Laptop computer

- ☐ Camera(s)
- ☐ Folding canvas chair
- ☐ Overnight clothes
- ☐ Hiking boots
- ☐ Swimsuit
- ☐ Water bottle
- ☐ Drinks
- ☐ Snacks

Typical Process

1. Quiet travel in the car or listen to a stimulating new audio book
2. Pray for blessing, give thanks, or be quiet
3. Document what did and did not work well for me over the recent past
4. Read some scripture
5. Assess how God is working in my life
6. Process, quiet, exercise
7. Read from a personal-growth book
8. Identify options for the balance of my retreat time

I've gained so much value from these times by ensuring I've dedicated the time and that I'm prepared with supplies and some level of structure for these "unstructured" Refocus Sessions.

Chapter 8

Structure Is
So Helpful

What happens when there is no structure? A lack of structure or cohesiveness can leave you feeling unsettled or scattered. I find that a book with poor structure is difficult to read. A teacher or speaker who jumps all over without structure is hard to follow and difficult to listen to and learn from. Music with no structure or coordination between the instruments or voices would not evoke feelings of joy, but rather be impossible to listen to. Structure is so helpful.

When I ask someone an extremely open-ended question, like "How are you?" or "What do you want?" it's difficult for them to access their thoughts in order to respond with any level of depth. Narrower questions are easier to respond to, like "What do you want to gain from reading *Refocus*?" More structure and some narrowing of the topic typically make it easier for us to think clearly and focus our attention successfully. I've discovered this also to be true in regard to Refocus Sessions.

To get some exercise, some days I walk on our neighborhood sidewalks to Lazelle Wood Park, which has a nice one-mile trail. This is a good option to get in a 45-minute walk. I see people with phones or headsets listening to something or talking with someone, multi-tasking to distract themselves while they exercise.

I usually walk in silence, taking in the sights around me as I travel my path. This can be enjoyable and refreshing, but having seen the same path over and over, it can get monotonous. When my mind wanders for an extended time without intentional focus I can get bored. If I select a topic or question to ponder during my walk, I get energized and gain fresh new ideas and perspectives. My time seems to fly by. I get home and can't believe my exercise time is already over. Giving my mind something to focus on changes everything.

Going off by yourself with paper and pen to spend three to eight hours just thinking might seem like it would be dull or tedious. What does it mean to just think? How do you start? What do you think about? How do you think about it? You might be saying to yourself, "I'm not going to do that. It would be hard, a waste of my time. And how could it even really help me?" If you're feeling this way, you're not alone. This process was an intriguing yet uncomfortable prospect for me years ago when I began my refocusing adventures to invest in the growth of myself. My process has evolved over the years and works well for me, and you will find elements of it that resonate well with you and ones that don't. That is okay! The hardest part is over-coming the inertia of your mind-talk that keeps you stagnant and locked into the frustration and comfort of the status quo.

In the following chapters I describe several options in regard to structure that should help you, not hinder you, in getting clearer and sharper about your life, what you're doing, what you want to do, and how you can better get there.

Chapter 9

Refocus Sessions

The Three Levels

I'm providing some options for Refocus Sessions that worked well for me – not THE option, or the one way you can refocus your life – so you don't have to invest the time I already have in thinking through, developing, and modifying your tools.

I developed three levels of Refocus Sessions. You can review them and decide which would be most beneficial for you. I define these levels in terms of depth, as of the ocean.

Some people live floating on the surface of a turbulent ocean, being tossed about by the large waves and strong winds on the surface. This is a tumultuous place to live, where you can easily get swept up by the tides that make it difficult to see clearly. Going deeper into what is happening below the surface, you find a place that is calmer, and the deeper you go the calmer it is. Going five feet deep into the ocean of your life represents the first level of Refocus Sessions. For the next level, you go 20 feet deep; and level three is going 50 feet deep into discovery about what is happening in your life. I believe all three levels provide terrific value. In the appendix I provide a form for each of the three levels.

The first level is a start and is quite simple – the Five Feet Deep version. It can provide wonderful value if you've never taken the time to stop and intentionally think about how you're doing and where you want to go. Each of the next two levels involves increasing the structure, content, and depth of the process. The Fifty Feet Deep level is where I refocus today, and has the most structure. It's a deep dive with a holistic viewpoint.

The Five Feet Deep Level

This is how I started my Refocus Sessions years ago. I only had a few guidelines, but even those few were extremely helpful. I loved these times and they resulted in positive changes and improvements in my life.

Be Away

First, I needed to be away from my standard living environment. It could be going to a park or to a Panera or some other restaurant, but it needed to be away from my familiar surroundings. Being away helps you see things in a new light with a different mindset, which allows you to get yourself out of any rut you might be in. I intentionally set aside specific time periods for these sessions – between three and eight hours, sometimes a little longer to include a night at a hotel or cabin.

What to Take

These items come from the checklist I shared earlier. If not going to a restaurant, I would usually take a folding canvas chair. I would take my Bible or my phone with my Bible application, perhaps a thought-provoking book I had been reading, plenty of blank paper, a couple of pens (in case I ran out of ink), a highlighter, a hard writing surface, a notebook, sunglasses, and finally, usually a hat with a good-sized brim or bill to protect my face from the sun.

Be Present

Once I was settled, I invested time in being fully present, enjoying where I was and taking the time to breathe, see, and appreciate all that was around me. This usually lasted anywhere from 10 to 30 minutes. When you stop and look, taking deep breaths, there is a lot to this creation, and it keeps going whether you pay attention or not. It provides context for seeing all that is going on around you while you're focused on you and your life.

Pluses and Minuses

Next I would pull out a blank page and draw a long line down the middle. I placed a large plus sign at the top of the left column and a large minus sign at the top of the right column. Then I was ready to address two high-level, open-ended questions: "What's going well in my life?" and "What isn't?"

I thought about my life and started to write right away. It didn't matter which column I started or ended with. Anything that came to mind was documented on my page in either the plus column (going well) or minus column (not going as well). I would do this for an hour or more. I wrote until my mind felt relatively empty, or I needed a break.

The "Going Well"

The "Going Well" notes provide context. You always have both good and bad occurring in life, and it's healthy and encouraging to spend time focusing on what's going well. I often had a lot of content in that column. It's easy to forget these things and take them for granted. By categorizing in this way, you gain a renewed sense of appreciation.

The "Not Going as Well"

Then I worked through the right column. I reviewed each item to determine what was in my control and what was just a fact of life. A simple example is cloudy or rainy days. They aren't in your control, so acknowledge them and move to the next item. Search for those things that are within your control. Underline a key word or two in each one.

Improvements

Next I brainstormed about things I could do to change or improve each of the situations in the minus or "Not Going as Well" column. Then I went back through them one more time, highlighting or circling two to four actions from the entire list to take seriously – ones that really resonated with me at that point in time. I tried to pick a reasonable and manageable number so as not to be overwhelmed but rather empowered that I was taking more control of my life and moving forward. Just the exercise of becoming more aware of things, writing them down, and thinking about them can help you transform them. You might identify 15 or more potential "to dos" in that right column, but limiting your focus to two to four of them that feel most important is enough, while the others can just become part of your background thinking.

Application

Then I made notes on another piece of paper about what actions I would take. I would enjoy the rest of my time, going for a short, slow, relaxing walk. Then I packed and headed home, energized that I would be doing many of the right things, had planned in order to do them well, and was living an unbelievably blessed life and had specific plans to improve important areas of my life.

When I got home I would use these notes to make some changes right away, and others I scheduled into my calendar for the most appropriate times.

Working on My Life

From the first time I tried this until today, I've treasured this time investment. For years it's benefited me, my family, and others. I've taken the time to honestly think and reflect about life, me, and where I'm headed. As an entrepreneur I've been encouraged to work "on my business, not just in my business." In a sense this is the same thing: working on your life, not just in your life.

I hope you will give the Five Feet Deep level a try and learn the value for yourself. Each of the next two levels builds on this first one. I won't repeat the basics of the first level in the descriptions below, but they are important parts of all of the levels.

The Twenty Feet Deep Level

Thanks Time

This level includes a specific "Thanks Time." This is taking the time to stop, think, and list the things you're thankful for. It's so easy to take things for granted. It's always valuable to stop, observe, and be thankful for what you have.

This can include specific things that have recently come to mind. For example, air conditioning if yours recently failed, or electricity if you recently lost yours for a few hours, or the US Postal Service if a recent three-day weekend extended the delivery of something you were hoping to receive.

I also include the basics of life: Clean air 24/7. Cool breezes. The availability of good, clean, healthy food. Lights in our home for the night times. Clean running water from multiple places inside our home – even hot if we want it. I'm so blessed with so much that it's easy to take it for granted. It's a fantastic investment to recall and be thankful for these things, making me feel grateful as I move to focusing on other topics.

Key Life Areas

Rather than thinking about what is going well and not so well in an open-ended way, which can be freeing but also intimidating for some, identify key aspects of your life and zero in on each area, one at a time, evaluating how things are going. This narrowing process can ensure that you've focused on the most important areas of your life. They can be defined and prioritized, depending on how many you come up with. My list started relatively small and has grown significantly, as you will see in the Fifty Feet Deep level.

Determine what is most important to you for this particular session. You might want to think about your body, soul, and spirit, one at a time. Maybe you opt for other life areas like food, exercise, family, relationships, work, hobbies, or whatever comes to mind. I encourage you to identify no more than eight life areas. (You'll see the additional areas I use when I introduce the Fifty Feet Deep level.)

Three Questions

Next ask yourself three key questions, the answers to which I've found to be quite insightful. As a life coach, I ask people two types of critical questions that can change their lives: questions they don't know they need to ask themselves, and questions they know they should ask themselves but don't want to, or won't. The three questions below probably fall into one of these two categories for you.

"What Should I Be Focusing On That I'm Not?"

Skim through what you consider to be the most important areas of your life and the biggest issues right now; you might be taking one or more of them for granted and assuming everything is fine. When these areas are going fine, you often don't give them a second thought. But without introspection they can become blind spots and keep you stuck in ineffective habits of doing and relating. It might be your health, or your relationships – especially your relationship with your spouse or significant other. Maybe it's your kids or the need to take vacation time away to relax and refresh. It can be anything. Keep an open mind in identifying one or more area of potential neglect and evaluate:

- How that area is going
- What is working well
- Are you intentionally investing in it?
- Is it delivering the results you want?
- What elements of this area aren't working well and might be creating the opposite of what you want?

Left unchecked, over time problems in these major life areas can creep up on you and jump you like a monster in the night, totally devastating you. So get the jump on that monster with this question.

"What Decision or Decisions Do I Need to Be Making That I'm Delaying?"

This question brings to mind issues that have been actively weighing on your mind — things that are dragging you down, making you feel low.

Once you've identified a topic or topics, you can shine a light on what you still need to learn about that topic, if anything, before making key decisions about it. This process directly impacts the results you will achieve. We so often remain stagnant due to the stories we create in our heads, fearing what will come from our decision or action. I'm often afraid of what I imagine might happen as a result of a decision I'm making, which is what makes this an excellent question for me. Taking the time to identify the topic, and then evaluating what is causing you to delay your decision, provide the push you need to make a decision or at least define a deadline for making it. What you're waiting on likely won't change the end result; you're just hesitating out of fear, and it drags you down like you're carrying a mound of bricks on your back, maybe for days, weeks, or months. Procrastination can add stress to your life, reducing how sharp you are in other areas. This question is a powerful motivator for action.

"What Do I Need to Say No To?"

This is a tough question that's hard to face. Once I've taken the time to assess how well things are going in the areas I consider most important, I can see more clearly that I might need to step away from certain activities that are not harming me but are deluding my focus and energy or spreading me too thin to accomplish more important things.

Sometimes it's more helpful to add things and other times it's more helpful to take things away. I have discovered that to be more effective we sometimes need to say no to things even more than we need to say yes to new things that we think will help us. Saying no is sometimes the most powerful thing you can do, so this is another powerful question to include in this assessment.

The Twenty Feet Deep level can provide a whole new level of discovery when you make the time, focus, and approach it with intention.

The Fifty Feet Deep Level

The Fifty Feet Deep level adds much value to the process, but also takes more time and concentration. It often takes me multiple sessions to complete this full and valuable process. This is the most complex and thought-provoking level. After having conducted personal Refocus Sessions for over two decades, this is now the level I engage in regularly.

You may find this level helpful if you're seasoned at taking personal time away to think. If not, choose a few parts that you feel would be most helpful and start with those. This level builds on the first two.

One key addition as I dive deeper is asking myself how God is working in my life. I also address more life areas. I include a word-picture element to prompt some creative thinking about my current state of mind. I coach myself regarding one topic that surfaced during the review of my life areas earlier in the session. I review and assess my annual goals. I evaluate how well I'm living one of my defined governing values. I review and assess recent journal entries, evaluating how well I've been applying what I've learned. Then I complete a 10-year forward-looking exercise. Finally I complete an "Application Matrix" in which I summarize the most important action items from the session to focus on.

Now I'll take you through each of these steps so you can see how helpful they might be for you.

How is God Currently Working in My Life?

I wanted to include a spiritual component early in this process, so addressing my current relationship with God became the first new component in the Fifty Feet Deep level. The question is stated this way: "How is God currently working in my life beyond the many basics He provides daily?"

I likely already addressed most of the basics during my "Thanks Time" (as in the Twenty Feet Deep level), so this broader question can result in a variety of different responses. My responses have included "He's revealing how much He's beyond comprehension, even just through what I see in creation"; "He desires that I improve the words I'm using"; and "He challenged me to do something different with, or for, Carolyn," and sometimes my responses have even been that I'm not seeing Him work in my life beyond providing the basics to live.

There isn't a "right" answer. The question is intended to help me think about how God has been dealing with me recently and to strengthen my relationship with Him. My views about how actively He's working to change me have shifted over the years.

Key Life Areas

The biggest addition of the Fifty Feet Deep level is the number of life areas I assess. The process is the same, but I look at more aspects of my life. As with the life areas covered in the first two levels, I list what is currently going well and what is not going well, and then define actions I would like to take to improve in each area. You can pick and choose the areas that are most relevant to you; nevertheless, I hope you find all the following 21 areas that I evaluate to be thought-provoking.

The Big Three

I start with a very high-level, broad perspective. The first three areas I assess are Spiritual, Body, and Soul.

Six Life Priorities

Then I assess the top priorities for me: Worship, Enjoyment, Experiences, Relationships, Learning, and Contribution. You will, of course, choose your own top priorities. One at a time, I think through and evaluate how I am living each of these from a global standpoint.

Other General Life Areas

Then I evaluate Family, Home/Maintenance, Play, Business/Work, Focus/Execution of Long-Term Goals, Management of Daily Energy and Tasks, Life Balance, and an "Other" category, in case there are additional things that come to mind during the session.

Operational Life Areas

Then I move to the operational side of my life, evaluating how well I'm leveraging my effectiveness and efficiency. I think through my time and energy; my clarity about my mission, vision, and current goals; how well I'm using structure and processes; and finally how I'm maintaining the things I possess.

This rounds out my list of 21 key life areas. This step can take up nearly half of my thinking time. These are areas I consider important to fulfillment in my life, so I don't want to take them for granted. I want to be sure I'm being clear and intentional about prioritizing and living each of them.

A Word Picture

"I'm hiking up a really fun, high mountain with many terrific views. I'm pretty much alone, like when I was at Juneau, Alaska. It's exciting and feels a little dangerous. I'm seeing views I've never seen before – they are amazing, beautiful, and inspirational. I'm really on my own. Carolyn is also hiking with me, but well below where I am. It's a fun and yet long and tiring journey. Others don't see what I'm seeing. I may not ever come down from this mountain. I'm peaceful, content, and thankful, and also disturbed that I might remain here, on my own, for a long time or permanently."

This is an entry from one of my Refocus Sessions that describes my feeling, in picture or story form, about where I was at that time.

Word pictures are a creative and fun element of my process. With this prompt, I think about how I see my life at that moment in relation to a real-life physical setting. It might be imagining I'm on the water, on a trail, or traveling on a road. I often find water analogies to be the most helpful.

I select a setting that best represents where I feel like I am, then I add detail to flesh out what I'm feeling. I've written about being in a small boat with no oars, in the middle of the ocean, as night falls, with dark clouds over my head and heavier clouds quickly blowing my direction. Other times I've written about gently floating with a few friends on a comfortable raft down a calm but moving river. We're traveling along with the sun brightly shining above us, and we feel a gentle breeze as we head to our destination.

Taking the time to describe myself in these settings often provides clarity about how I'm feeling and good insights about how well I'm doing or what I need to do to put myself in a better place. Give this a try and see if it can be as helpful for you.

I Coach Myself

Being a coach, I incorporate a self-coaching process into this level. I pick a topic that surfaced earlier in the session that lends itself well to self-coaching. I follow the routine coaching process: identify a topic, clearly define what you want in regard to that topic, note what you've tried and how it's worked, identify multiple options to improve the situation, and finally select one or more actions you can commit to in order to move forward.

I employ the whole coaching process and push myself on each of these steps. Self-coaching doesn't provide the benefits of another curious person helping you dive deep into your thinking, but you do still gain significant value and clarity from taking yourself through these steps.

Even if you're not familiar with the coaching process, you can follow the steps listed above and see if they provide value for you.

Annual Goals

Next I review my annual goals, one by one, assessing how well I've made progress, or not, and identifying any actions or behavioral changes I need to make.

It's powerful to establish annual goals, but it's much more powerful to regularly review them, assess your performance to date, and reconfirm or recommit to following through on them or determine new actions you need to take to move forward on your original plan, accelerate your plan, or modify it. The greatest power is in conducting regular reviews and assessments, and hopefully celebrating as you complete interim milestones.

Governing Values

As I shared earlier, years ago I established my personal governing values. In this step I select one of those values and think through whether I am or am not living it consistently. As with the other assessments, additional actions to start, stop, intensify, or reduce one or more of my behaviors can come from doing this.

As with goals, while it's valuable to establish your governing values, it's much more powerful to regularly review them, assessing your lifestyle and behavior relative to them. You'll continually grow in more alignment with them day by day and month by month throughout your life.

Journal Review

In chapter 12 I discuss my daily journaling process. In the Fifty Feet Deep level I review my recent daily journal entries. The entries can span a couple of weeks to a month or more. I focus primarily on the "lessons learned" section, reviewing the insights I gained on how to improve my life. This review shows me how well I've been applying what I learn each day. It can be encouraging or discouraging. It can be the kick in the pants I need to be more dedicated to a change I want or need to make. This step generates even more value from my daily journaling investment.

Look 10 Years Out

Now I take a long view and project where I will potentially be and what I will likely accomplish if I stay on my current path continually doing the same things. I also think through how adjustments I make now might impact my results 10 years out.

It's sometimes difficult to remember that the actions you take today are like bricks being stacked up to build your future. Taking the time to think through and imagine your future results helps motivate you to be even more committed to the important actions you need to be taking. It helps you remember that the little things you do each day add up to create the big things that will happen in your future, both to your benefit and to your detriment.

This is a challenging step because it's hard to project the future 10 years from now. It's also an energizing step because of the potential of your future if you maintain and enhance your best and healthiest routines and behaviors.

Give it a try. See what surfaces. Can you see what you could be in 10 years? Does it bring a smile or a frown to your face? What do you need to do today to make it a great big grin?

Application Matrix

To gain clarity on the most important tangible points from the whole session, I finish by completing a four-box matrix summarizing the key changes I want to focus on making:

Stop doing	Start doing
Do less	Do more

This simple structure provides excellent clarity for actionable steps that will propel me forward to greater personal growth. I start at the top of my notes from the session, looking for key actions I want to pull out for this matrix. When I find something I really want to prioritize, I write it in the appropriate box. In the "Do more" box I might write, "Use alarm five days a week to wake by 7:10 a.m." This might be tied to a critique I made of myself about sleeping in too often. I might write in the "Start doing" box, "Play guitar three days a week." Ideally I choose four to 10 actions that I would like to apply moving forward.

This step makes it easier in the days ahead to quickly review the key results from the Refocus Session. The thinking is good, but the real power comes from doing something with that thinking to better align your life and behaviors with the ideal life you want. The actions are what change your life. When nothing changes, nothing changes. If you want to change or improve, you must take action on your Refocus Sessions.

This is the Fifty Feet Deep level. Although it takes time and mental energy to complete this detailed process, you will come away more confident in who you are, where you have been going, and what you need to reinforce or change to help you move even more directly toward your ideal future. I hope whatever elements of the process you choose to practice help you move toward that future.

Chapter 10

Creativity, Application, and Results

Creativity

It can feel intense as you concentrate for hours on the topics of your Refocus Session. Below are a few simple ways to incorporate creativity into this robust process.

Draw a Picture

Sometimes doodling or drawing for a while can be freeing and move you into more of a free-flowing, creative thinking process. Give it a try using one of the themes you're thinking through. It might be your food consumption, how you're investing your time, your morning wake-up routine, or any topic that surfaced during your session. Or just draw what comes to mind when you feel stuck. Drawing and doodling can provide additional clarity about what's happening or perhaps what you would like to have happen.

Mindstorming

Here's a powerful bonus exercise. It's what author and speaker Brian Tracy calls "mindstorming." It's a fantastic concept that I've shared and used with coaching clients. The process is like climbing a ladder; it helps you step up to a higher level of thinking.

You've probably heard of brainstorming, in which a group of people generates a bunch of ideas and documents them on a chalk board (do they still exist?), flip chart, or some type of electronic device. Mindstorming is basically brainstorming with yourself. Jot down every possible solution to a problem, or all the ways you could accomplish a dream or a goal. Do this until you've identified at least 20 options. This can take a lot of time and effort, but it's quite rewarding. I've been able to successfully reach at least 20 options every time I've used this process.

I offered mindstorming to a client a few years ago and he said, "Yes, I want to try it." At our next session he reported that he didn't get 20 options – in this case 20 reasons why he was feeling so much more energy since I had been coaching him. I was surprised and a little disappointed until he shared, "I couldn't stop. I came up with thirty-three reasons!" As you can imagine, this response brought a big smile to my face. He summed up his assessment: "In the end, to summarize these thirty-three reasons, I'm taking control of my life again and it feels so good!"

As you face various obstacles, challenges, and problems, I encourage you to try mindstorming. To get to 20 or more options you'll likely have to raise your current level of thinking. Think outside your normal – outside the box. Include some crazy ideas that make no immediate sense to you. Just let it flow.

Mindstorming forces you to continually think at a new and creative level and cross new thresholds in your mind. It feels so good when you push through and your mind is thinking at a whole new level. After listing a few options, you might think you've thought of everything possible and that there are no new solutions; but I assure you, there are more. When you feel your creativity and flow is blocked, push through and keep listing. This blocked feeling may happen again and again, maybe at solution number 13, and then again at 18. Keep going and feel your mind expand.

Once you have at least 20 options, the challenge is to select one or two actions that you can tangibly take to move forward in addressing that problem or goal. Combining multiple options often creates a fantastic new solution. Perhaps combining options 2, 14, and 18 into one new idea gives you a creative solution for moving forward.

You can find out more about mindstorming by googling it. Brian Tracy describes the concept in more detail in some of his books, including *No Excuses*.

Give it a try the next time you face a problem or issue or you're stuck on how to achieve a goal. It can create stimulating new ideas that were lying dormant inside you the whole time.

Identify an Image

Think through an image of something that reflects where you are today or maybe where you want to be. This can be experienced-based, like the word-picture step in the Fifty Feet Deep level of the Refocus Session; or you might picture an object: What is it and how does it work? How is it maintained, and what doesn't it do well? Some examples are a kite, a hammer, a chisel, a bicycle, and a chair.

Maybe you want to feel more confident and rock-solid than you feel today, so you might visualize a sturdy chair, how it's constructed, what makes it most helpful, how it's back is supported, how high the seat is, and what it can do for you. Does it have four legs or fewer? How thick and solid are the legs? How long are they and how close are they to one another? Relate each of these points to you and your current situation. What would you be like if you were the chair? What would you want it to look like? What do you need to change to be the chair you want to be?

I've found analogies like these helpful in finding creative ways to improve my current setting, environment, and behaviors. If it sounds intriguing or interesting, give it a try.

Write a Poem or Song

If you're naturally creative, you might want to take it to a more extreme level. Write a new poem or song. Create a new tune. Maybe do both and combine them. As long as you're by yourself, sing it out loud, meditating on the flow of the tune or the words of your poem; there's no one around to criticize. Being creative in this way can be freeing if you have the guts and confidence to try it.

Sing a Familiar Song

Sometimes a familiar song comes to mind while you think through a topic. Go ahead and pause and sing it to yourself, and think about the words. It might help as you think through where you are and what you want.

For example, if you're thinking about how you spend your valuable time, the "Cat's in the Cradle" song by Harry Chapin might help you think it through. Or if you're facing a mountain of tasks it might be helpful to sing and think through the words of the Jefferson Starship song "Miracles." Sing a few of the lines, over and over, and imagine the future you want.

Songs can be powerful and freeing. You might have experienced this while singing in the shower, thinking no one was home. For your sake I hope you were right and you didn't have to face a critique from someone just because you wanted to enjoy letting go and boldly blurting out the words of a fun song.

Do Something Physical

One way to break out of a rut, whether it's a physical rut or a thinking rut, is to move your body – the more creatively the better. You can go for a walk, jump up and down, take some long strides during a walk, hang and swing from the limb of a tree, or swing your arms left and right as far as you can, letting your waist twist and turn with your movement. Just about any movement that is not routine, normal, and natural for you can inject new energy and free your body and mind to move to a new level. And it doesn't require much time. You can perform any of these movements for 10 or 15 seconds and be amazed by how much different it makes you feel and think. Give it a try when you're feeling stuck.

I hope these examples are helpful. There are also many more things you can do to bring creativity into your Refocus Sessions. Try whatever comes to mind if it helps move you forward in your thinking.

Application

It's beneficial to invest in thinking time, which can be stimulating and enjoyable in itself; but the real goal is meaningful change and improvement for you and those you love and touch. I've discovered several ways to bring my thinking to fruition with tangible results and an intentionally lived life.

Immediate Changes

Some of these strategies can be implemented immediately, such as discontinuing something you're doing that's hindering progress, taking something off your calendar or to-do list, and adding something that you'll take action on in the next day or so. I write a separate note and put it on my study desk to ensure that I see it and take action. I don't want to have to flip through 10 or 15 pages of notes to find a particular action item. These actions are the most rewarding because you get to see results right away. On occasion there are even things you can do, stop doing, or change *during* your Refocus Session.

Application Matrix

I often pull out the page with my Application Matrix on it and rotate it through my daily to-do lists for a few weeks to keep those actions top of mind so I can apply them in my daily life. Anything I can do to place my new decisions in front of my eyes on a frequent basis helps me follow through.

Checklists

At times I've created checklists to help me implement my new actions. It can be a daily checklist to track how much water or liquid I'm drinking, the number of days a week I'm waking early, or how much soda I'm consuming during the week.

I move the checklist from day to day with my to-do list; or, if it's something I really want to increase my focus on, I make a separate note and leave it on my desk for several days or weeks until I've either completed the action or established a solid new habit. It has been said that it takes 21 days to form a daily habit. Repeating an action for three or four weeks has often allowed me to build a new habit. And tracking it in writing definitely improves my performance.

Accountability Partner

There have been times when I couldn't seem to limit how often I ordered French fries – one of my favorites; couldn't get myself to consistently exercise five days a week; wasn't noticing and appreciating Carolyn as I would like to; wasn't planning my days each morning as consistently as I would like to; or wasn't drinking as much water as I know I should. If I'm not doing something well on my own, enlisting an accountability partner can really help, and I've had several throughout my life.

First verbalize, or at least write specifically, what you want help with. This takes boldness that is well beyond establishing a goal in your mind or in your private documents. Taking this step provides additional clarity because you have to write it down clearly enough for your partner to understand it. Stating the goal out loud is powerful.

Although it can make you feel vulnerable to have someone ask you how you're doing on a goal, it increases your commitment and allows for someone to encourage you and celebrate with you as you make progress toward your goals. Selecting the right person gives you a whole new level of support as you work to accomplish your goal.

Results

What has come from these time investments? So much! I've already shared how these are freeing and enjoyable times. They increase my motivation and confidence in my decisions and actions. They generate different and better results than I was previously experiencing.

It's amazing that when you make a change in your life, and it becomes your new routine, you seem to forget that you ever lived a different way. Reviewing my past notes helps me celebrate the new, different, better, and stronger person I've become. In several ways I'm a new man. I joke with Carolyn that I'm not the man she married over 40 years ago; but I'm the same guy, and I'm better, stronger, and have achieved so much more than I could have as the person she first married. I would even dare to say I'm significantly different from the man I was even five or 10 years ago. I continue to grow and change, making improvements as I gain more experience, knowledge, and wisdom. I believe everything compounds when you invest in learning and growing. Here are a few examples from my life:

Life can be hard and it can drag you down. My Refocus Sessions have made me realize that when life is a drag I need to jump back in control of it and not let important things slide, such as refocusing on my diet, going to bed earlier, consistently waking earlier, reading to improve myself, reaching out to friends I've neglected, planning for my day the night before so I start the next morning more productively, reducing the amount of TV I watch, and much more.

I've started or stopped many things as a result of Refocus Sessions. These include stopping participating in a church group that wasn't clicking; looking for better, stronger, encouraging relationships, like finding the Worthington book club hosted by Josh Jordan; increasing my focus on the net income from my business; stopping physical therapy that was no longer helpful; reducing my engagement in mentorship after having gained much of what I could get from it; scheduling weekly date times with Carolyn; stopping sleeping beyond eight hours on a regular basis, which can easily happen when you're retired; offering to go on more walks with Carolyn when she's exercising; and contacting my parents more frequently when they were going through some rough health issues. I've made many changes. They aren't all earth shattering, but each of them has helped move me closer to being the person I would like to be.

I hope these few examples are encouraging. It's easy for life to get busy and carry you downstream, away from what you deem important, and I'm excited about the value Refocus Sessions can bring to your life, too.

Additional
Refocus Tools

Chapter 11

The State of Me – The Spider Diagram

Sometimes I feel overwhelmed and I want more context about where I am and what's going on right now. Everything seems harder when I can't see how what I'm doing fits into the whole of me. This feeling slows me down and crushes my motivation. I want a quick snapshot of my life and to review its current context without taking the time to conduct a Refocus Session.

I've discovered a solution that gets me back on track and moving forward but isn't as time-consuming as a Refocus Session. It's a simple, hand-scribbled diagram about my life and its context. The end product looks like a spider web, with each of my current activities tied together into one full picture of my life activities. It helps me see, on one sheet, all I have going on, and allows me to quickly evaluate areas in which I'm frustrated, that need more attention, that need to be dropped, or that need to be put on the back burner.

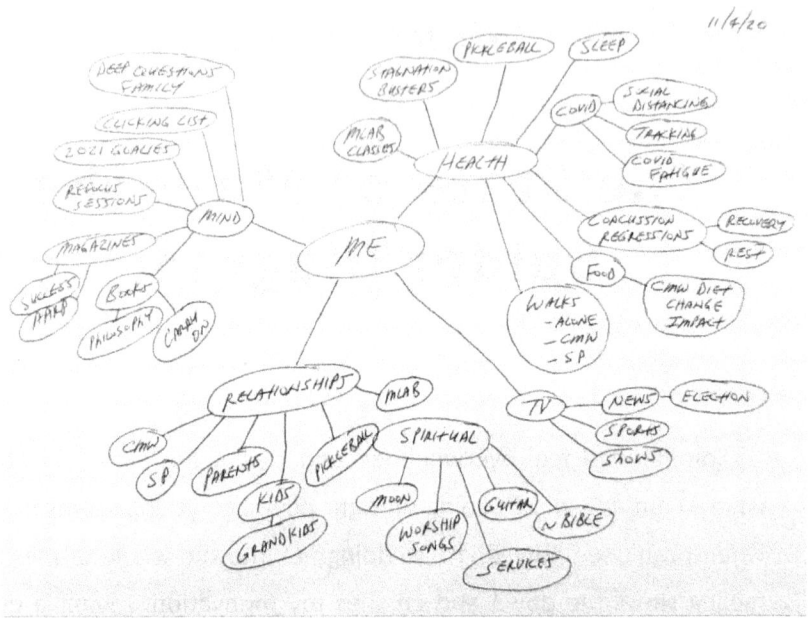

Major Segments

I start by writing "Me" in the middle of the page. Then I list the major segments of my life in a circle around the Me. These topics vary based on what I have going on at the time, but I often begin with the basics of life like Health, Spiritual, Work, Home, Relationships, Pleasure, and several others. Then I connect each of these to the Me in the middle by drawing lines to the center.

Related Activities

Then I list the activities related to each of the segments until I've covered all the key ways in which I'm currently investing my time. For example, my list regarding Health might have the subcategories Ninja, Walking, Pickleball, and what I call "Stagnation Busters." Under Ninja I might list MLab Ohio open gyms, Ninja competitions, Ninjaing at local parks, and Hanging on obstacles at home.

Once I've fleshed out each of the segments I have a relatively full picture of how I'm spending my time right now – what I'm apparently considering important.

Assessment

Next I conduct a broad-picture review from a number of different angles. I ask myself, "Am I involved in too much right now? Is there something I'm missing that I really should be doing or would like to be doing?" Then I evaluate how much time I'm spending in each area. I usually do this in my head, but you can certainly add notes to the diagram. I mentally review each item and determine whether I'm spending too much, too little, or about the right amount of time in that area. From these assessments I decide whether I need to make changes. I might elect to stop doing several things, at least for a while, or add something, or make other tweaks in how I'm living. I often put my spider diagram in my calendar file, reviewing it once a week for a month or so.

Having this document on file can be very helpful while I'm adjusting my schedule over the next few days or weeks.

Chapter 12

Daily Journaling

The October/November 2020 issue of *AARP The Magazine* included an article titled "Life Lessons from the Queen," reflecting the perspective of 94-year-old Queen Elizabeth. A subsection – "Stick to a Schedule" – included the following: "From her first day as queen, Elizabeth has calmed her mind by following a strict daily regimen, ending each day by writing in her journal." She is just one example of a prominent person who writes (or wrote) daily in their journal. It seems to be a very valuable practice, and the time I spend journaling each day has become a tremendous reflection time as well.

Over the years I was motivated by various books and teachings to journal about my days. I would try it for a time but eventually get tired of it. I didn't see any real benefit other than that I was doing what people I respected said was a good thing to do. So I would start and stop, and it never really took hold. I felt like I needed to write about every event and activity of my day, which could take up to an hour. It took too much time for the value I received from it. If I went back and read my entries, it was helpful as documentation, but that was it. And that wasn't enough of a payback to motivate me to stay with it. I journaled regularly three different times over the years, but always stopped.

A few years ago that changed in a significant way. I came across an article in the May 2015 *Success* magazine that encouraged readers to try journaling again if they had tried it in the past but couldn't stay with it. The article intrigued me, as it encouraged readers to simply write a few sentences about the key experiences or feelings for the day. It said a journal entry could be as short as one sentence. This was vastly different from the two to three pages and 40 to 60 minutes I had felt committed to in the past. This was a freeing new concept.

I decided to give it a try again, and I found the few short minutes to be a helpful reflection time each day. I usually completed it at the end of the day or, at the latest, early the next morning. I discovered that when I went through this process at night, the events of the day were much fresher in my mind.

As I have continued to appreciate and even enjoy this reflection process, I have let it take more time and grow into longer entries. I made sure I was focused on the time I was spending, not letting it take over but using it as a tool to help me think through, learn from, and appreciate the day.

Over time I believed that adding structure would be helpful, so I incorporated various elements into each entry. Now it generally takes between 15 and 20 minutes. Sometimes it can take nearly 30 minutes when I get absorbed in the thought-provoking process. Some days it only takes eight to 10 minutes.

Below I take you through my current process. I encourage you to try the elements that seem like they'll be of most value to you. Experiment with them. As I did, start by writing just a few simple sentences.

Purpose

The primary value I gain from journaling comes from reflecting and thinking about my day, ensuring that no day is a lost day but rather is appreciated and learned from. It's the thought process that is most beneficial. The documentation can be helpful when I look back at my entries during my Refocus Sessions, but even if I experience only the mental review, I gain over 60 percent of the value. The writing process adds clarity, so it probably contributes 30 percent of the remaining value. That last 10 percent is the value of being able to look back and learn about some portion of my prior life. The time spent reflecting is clearly the most valuable part of the process.

When

As I mentioned, I usually journal right before going to bed when I'm not rushed and I'm finished with the meaningful activity of my day. When I'm very tired, or up late with an activity, I push the journaling to the next day, early in the morning, but it's amazing how much I lose when I wait till the next morning. By then I'm rested, refreshed, and into my next day. So much of the feeling and emotion from the prior day are gone. Looking through my to-do list for the prior day helps me remember what I did and can lead to some memory about my feelings, but it's not the same as when I take the time the prior night. I write my entries that same night about 90 percent of the time.

Where and on What

I write in a variety of places, maybe sitting in my study, maybe in the recliner in our guest bedroom, or sometimes lying on my belly in bed. The where is not as important as just doing it, and when. Try to be comfortable and not rushed.

I usually write in a formal bound journal or a spiral notebook. You can use a legal pad, notebook paper, a phone, tablet, or computer. Use what works best for you.

Seven Elements

Again, structure simplifies the process and makes it easier to ensure that you're focusing on the things that are most important to you. Over time your process may grow or decrease based on what serves you best at that time. Try the elements below that sound most helpful. You can add or take away elements over time as you see fit.

I started this version of simple journaling over five years ago. Month by month, and year by year, I added to and refined it. Today my journaling process consists of four major segments and three ratings. The segments are: a summary of the day; a statement about what I *should* be saying to myself in my self-talk (in contrast to what I *am* saying to myself); a "lessons learned" segment; and finally a "thanks" segment. There might be other key areas you want to include in your journaling, but these work well for me.

Sandwiched between these segments are the ratings. They're based on a scale of 1 to 10, 10 being the best. I evaluate how I feel I used the day – 1 being very poorly and 10 being very well. I also evaluate how well I invested the day, meaning whether or not I did things that will benefit the future – mine and others'. Finally I evaluate how well I focused on God during the day.

These are the key elements of my journaling process. I use various formats or notations so that at a quick glance I can skim my journal and quickly tell how I rated the day. I can also read the detail about any of the four segments. The most important thing is that I thought through each of the seven elements.

Below is a simple diagram of this process; then I describe each element. I start by writing the date and the day of the week at the top of the entry.

Daily Journaling Outline

Write about the key experiences and feelings of my day.

On a scale of 1-10, rate how well I lived the day.

Write what I should be saying to myself.

On a scale of 1-10, rate how well I invested my day for the future.

Write what I have learned from the day.

On a Scale of 1-10, rate how well I focused on God.

Write about what I'm thankful for from the day.

Key Experiences and Feelings of the Day

This is a free-form segment. I think and write about how the day went, noting any special or unique events or activities. I often comment about how well I slept. Since suffering a concussion in 2018, I've had a lot of hard nights. My sleep has a significant impact on how I live and invest in my day. Sometimes I provide a sleep rating and circle it. An 8: "Yay! I slept so much better," or a 2: "Wow, I lay awake in bed till almost 4:00 a.m. trying to fall asleep." You might have a different health issue or something else that you would like to track, such as your blood pressure or how much you exercised.

I usually list my key activities, like "I wrote and reviewed another chapter of my book" or "I cooked a meal for us, which took 90 minutes, but turned out well." I might write about someone I spoke to or a nice walk I went on.

I try hard to include the emotions I felt during the day, be it a victorious feeling as I pushed through my commitment to dust the house, or a feeling of frustration that I couldn't get the energy and motivation to exercise. It might be the excitement I felt from a video call I had with a group that was stimulating during a tough time. Sometimes it's the discouragement I feel because I had nothing left in me after a busy day and spent the evening watching TV.

I try to not focus on details, but sometimes I document details about an unusual event that I might want to refer to later or that evoked a particular emotion.

I often reference my to-do list. With some, hopefully most, or even all of the items crossed off, it helps jog my memory about what I did during the day. When I've completed this segment, I have a summary of how the day went. (I often complete my to-do list for the next day after doing my journal entry.)

How Well I Lived the Day (Rating)

How well did I use my day and how do I feel about it? Having the key activities top of mind, I might give myself a 4 if I feel like I really didn't do much or push through on things that I probably should have. A 4, or even less, might surface when I'm recovering from a concussion relapse. Certain situations continue to set me back, and the best I can do is lie down and rest all day, trying to regain strength and focus. Those days are usually rated low. They're "get by" days. I let my body heal while I'm patient and wait.

Some days I give myself an 8 or 9. I don't know that I've ever given myself a 10. That seems like too perfect of a day. Maybe I've had a 10, but I'm not sure I would give myself a 10 even if I had. An 8 or a 9 might mean that I pushed through and did several things that I didn't want to do or dreaded doing. It might reflect that I had an enjoyable time with others, positively influencing them. It might reflect a great day of both planning ahead and being disciplined enough to execute my plan. Higher ratings can come from a combination of good results across various aspects of my life.

Rating myself makes me evaluate and face the facts of the day. What was it really like, tangibly? Putting a number on it forces me to truly see it as it was. How well did I live the past 24 hours? Did I invest it well or waste it? I won't live forever, and I'm responsible for how well I live each day, be it in enjoyment of what I've been provided, contributing to others, or being responsible for what I've committed to. This is a helpful segment of my process.

I circle this number so I can quickly identify it when reviewing past entries.

What I Should Be Saying to Myself?

When I added this segment it brought a great deal of power to my process. I often treat myself like an enemy, saying negative, critical things to myself without even noticing. It feels natural, normal, and… negative. Answering this question has had a remarkable impact.

I've discovered that days that seem long and hard, and yet I push through them, are actually pretty good days. These include days when I pushed through on something I dreaded or feared and days when I contributed to someone else in a positive way even though it wasn't fun for me at the time.

When I ask what I should be saying to myself I often hear from my "best friend" – the kind, loving, supportive side of me that is often hidden. I know I should be saying things like "Way to go!" "You pushed through!" "You made a big impact today!" "You did things to improve your future!" "You did things to improve someone else's future," and "You stayed in bed and rested, which is what you needed today as you recovered from a concussion relapse."

Positive self-talk is a very powerful way to ensure you're seeing the bright side of things, and it shapes your entire perspective. You're hearing from a helpful inner friend – the balanced and optimistic side of you. You can emerge from this segment feeling much better about your day. A day doesn't have to feel enjoyable and fun to be a good day, as long as you can maintain a positive attitude going forward. I wish I could remember this better throughout my day, but at least I get this reminder and perspective before I go to bed, which can set the tone for some excellent sleep.

Sometimes my answer is a bit of a rebuke: "You need to stop eating French fries as often"; "You're staying up too late"; or a variety of other things. It's interesting that when I stop to answer this question I know I should be saying positive things to myself, but I seldom do so during the day. This segment helps move me in that direction.

[I enclose this entire segment in brackets, like the ones around this sentence, as its identifier.]

How Well I Invested My Day for the Future (Rating)

I want the mindset of *investing* in my days, not *spending* them, and this evaluation helps me remain in this mindset.

A 10 represents excellent actions that should significantly impact my future. It might be something memorable with Carolyn; writing a part of a book that will help others in the future, like this one; reading stimulating material that sharpened my perspective; or contributing to someone else in a way that will help them in the future by sharing an analogy or a quote or teaching them a new skill or mindset. It might be deciding not to spend money on something I've really wanted but which would have a poor return on investment or which I might use only a little or for a short period of time. Many things can result in a high rating.

On the other hand, a 2 or 3 would be a day that was spent just getting through the day or primarily on pleasure – fine for today but not much use for the future. Some pleasures generate great memories that will serve me well in the future, so days spent that way get a little higher rating, but other pleasures don't. A low rating can reflect a day of being lazy and unmotivated, or spending time waiting on something – or as some people say, "killing time." I don't like that phrase or attitude. I don't want that for me.

Taking the time to think about how I've invested in the future is an intentional and positive way to ensure, or at least potentially improve, my future. This is an important component of my journaling.

I draw a triangle around this number to identify it.

What I've Learned from the Day

For this segment I start by writing two capital *L*s – for "Lessons Learned," followed by a dash, like this: "LL–." I circle that to make it easy to find when looking back at past entries.

This segment takes me to the practical side of my experience. So far I've reviewed and evaluated how the day has gone, what has happened, what choices I've made, and the results that have come from them. This step goes beyond just the experiences. I explore what I will take away from today that will help me become a better, stronger person tomorrow and in the future.

This helps me focus on the highs and lows. What did I do to create the high points of the day? And further, how can I reinforce those behaviors and situations to create more of them? I want to cement them in my mind and reinforce those habits. For the lows, what went wrong or what was less than ideal? What could I have done to take more responsibility and make it better? This is, in a sense, my "do-over" time – a second chance. I get to look at an experience more objectively, from a wider view, after the fact, knowing what the results were. I get to analyze the situation and determine whether I might have done something to cause the negative result. I can almost always find at least one thing I could have done differently.

This is where those who feel like victims say to themselves, "It just happened to me. There was nothing I could have done differently." And they usually do this in a split second, without much thought. This is a terrible mindset that results in the same or similar poor results, over and over.

> *Insanity is doing the same thing over and over again and*
> *expecting different results.*
> *—generally attributed to Albert Einstein*

> *If nothing changes... nothing changes.*
> *—Avery Johnson*

These quotes are so true! This segment of my journaling provides the opportunity to change something, to make it better. I identify at least two or three things I could have thought better about or done better. It's amazing that I can repeatedly think poorly or do something poorly day in and day out even after 64 years on this Earth.

This is the most practical segment and it's the one I'm most likely to go back and review.

How Well I Focused on God (Rating)

This is the most recent addition to my journaling process. A 10 might mean that I took time early in the morning to be quiet before God, appreciating Creation as I looked out the window; meditated on a song of worship to God; or read my Bible or some other spiritually focused material. I might have spent time in nature, maybe on a walk or sitting in one of our antigravity chairs in the front yard, appreciating what God has created — from the immense sky and clouds to the details of the grass by my feet — being in awe of how it's designed and works together. It might be that I worshipped God by playing my guitar. Or I might have had a discussion about spiritual beliefs with Carolyn or a friend. These can all contribute to a high rating.

A low score is pretty easy to detect. I went through life mindlessly doing chores or just what was in front of me, not appreciating our world beyond what was around me. A rushed day is often a low-rated day. I need to take time to stop, observe, and appreciate to climb the scale toward a 10 in this category.

I write my rating number and then surround it with a box. Again, this is a different shape that helps me quickly find my spiritual evaluation.

What I'm Thankful For from the Day

Finally, I close with thanks. Maybe it should be first, but for now it remains the last element of my journal entry, after I've thought through everything else relative to my day. I indicate this element by writing a big, bold, white-in-the-middle *T*, followed by a dash, like this:

$$\mathbb{T}\text{-}$$

I list anywhere from two to 10 things that I'm thankful for today. This can include the basics that God provides miraculously every day, like the sun, the clean air, the ability to breathe, my restful sleep, the shade from a tree, the breeze blowing through the leaves or across my face, and even the rain. I know it's a weakness on my part, but I seldom remember to thank him for the clouds that so often fill our

Columbus, Ohio, sky. I should be more thankful for them; they provide many functions for us and the earth.

I might also list unique things from the day, like an especially fun experience with Carolyn; a special meeting with a friend; significant progress on reading or writing a book; an opportunity to explore a new place, maybe a park or restaurant; the ability to have a break away from home; or eating out somewhere special. The sky is the limit. There is almost no limit to what I could be thankful for on any particular day, but I simply document the first few things that come to mind. It's a fantastic way to end both my journal entry and my day.

Done for the Day

I close out the day by drawing a line across the page following my last sentence. This is a declaration that I'm done with today. It also makes it easy to flip through the pages and see when each day begins and ends. Then I write the date and day of the week for the next day's entry. It's helpful when reviewing my entries to know the date, but also the day of the week I experienced those things and felt that way.

Three Levels

Just as with Refocus Sessions, below I provide three levels of journaling to consider.

Five Feet Deep

Spend five to 10 minutes thinking about your day, and maybe briefly writing about it. Many do not even take this step on a regular basis.

Twenty Feet Deep

Write about your day, identifying two or three areas that you consider to be important. You can set up and stick to a short structure for this if you want to be sure to write about certain elements each day. They can be things you're thankful for, things you've learned, or things that moved you closer to your goals. The elements of my structure may not be the most important elements for you.

Fifty Feet Deep

The outline I described above is the Fifty Feet Deep level. You can replace some of the segments or ratings with other topics that are more important to you. This level requires a 10- to 30-minute investment of time each day. If you receive significant value, stay with it. If not, simplify it, but from my perspective not doing it at all is a poor choice if you want to have a better future than you're living today, even if today is good.

I hope this overview about my daily journaling process has been thought-provoking and helpful. If you've never journaled or haven't done so in a long time, start with the Five Feet Deep level and slowly move your way up the ladder if and when you feel it will be of value. I highly encourage you to give some level of it a try and watch as you become more reflective, more thankful, wiser, and an even better steward of your life.

Results

The greatest result from taking the time to journal is that it forces me to stop, take a breath, review, observe, learn, and frame my mindset toward appreciation – every day. This is such a change of pace from most everything else in my day. I see things clearly at least once each day.

I've also made numerous changes in my life based on what I discovered while journaling. Some were big deals and some were minor tweaks or modifications to my thinking or actions. Here are some examples from just this year:

Gaining Productivity

From May 22nd of 2020: I was sleeping in until 9:00 a.m. or later, costing me much in productivity. I was wasting what has often been my most productive time of the day. Since noting this in that journal entry, I've used my alarm more consistently and have set it for a much earlier time. I also created a group that exercised together early in the morning four days a week. That group helped me get up earlier on a more consistent basis, and I've been significantly more productive since then.

Allergies and More Stories

On June 5th, 2020, I wrote that I must look into options for my apparent new allergies. I was sneezing a lot when I was outside, though I had not had allergies in the past. I had to face the fact that I now had allergies. As a result I sought out medication that helped significantly. In the past I would have tried to push through something like that, never facing the fact that my body might have changed. I needed support that I hadn't needed in the past. This was a big change.

On that day I also learned that I should add more stories and feelings to the books I write to make them even more interesting. I learned this through reading *Stories That Stick* by Kindra Hall.

Reaching Potential

On July 18th, 2020, I wrote that I really like to see potential reached. That day I witnessed a competition in which a popular competitor wasn't able to perform to their potential. I was disappointed for them, and it hit me how excited I get when I see someone reach their potential in a specific event. I'm now more dedicated to stretching and growing to reach my potential. I try to model this and encourage it in others as well.

Transparency

With that journal entry it also hit me how transparent and honest I'm being in another book I'm currently writing about my recent spiritual journey. In it I'm revealing things that I hardly even knew about myself until I wrote them down. Documenting these is a scary exercise. It's one thing to think about things that scare you; it's a whole other thing to write them down where others can see them. I was encouraged that I was being honest, which came from investing quality time to journal about my day.

Chapter 13

Life Assessment Wheel

What is a life assessment wheel? Many coaches use various forms of assessment wheels to help clients see where they are in life and to help determine what the client should focus on as they attempt to move forward in their life. I've seen a lot of them and have used several. While they are helpful, I found that most are so simple that they don't provide as much value for my clients as they could.

Many assessment wheels have you rate the areas of your life, such as your health, career, etc., on a scale – for example from 1 to 10. But I found that when my clients first took the time to define what a 10 would look like for them, they often then rated themselves lower than they would have without that guideline. So I developed a tool that helps someone do that before giving themselves a rating. For each life category, you write in the wedge of the wheel for that category, using as many words as possible, what a 10 would look like for you, then move to the rating portion of the exercise.

I also expanded the number of categories to 12. Many assessment wheels only use five to seven categories. I wanted myself and my clients to think through and evaluate the additional categories of legacy, life pace, character, and adventure/recreation. I encourage clients to drop or replace any categories that aren't important to them. Most clients have used all the categories in my expanded assessment wheel.

Below is a blank Well Done Life (the name of my business) Life Assessment Wheel.

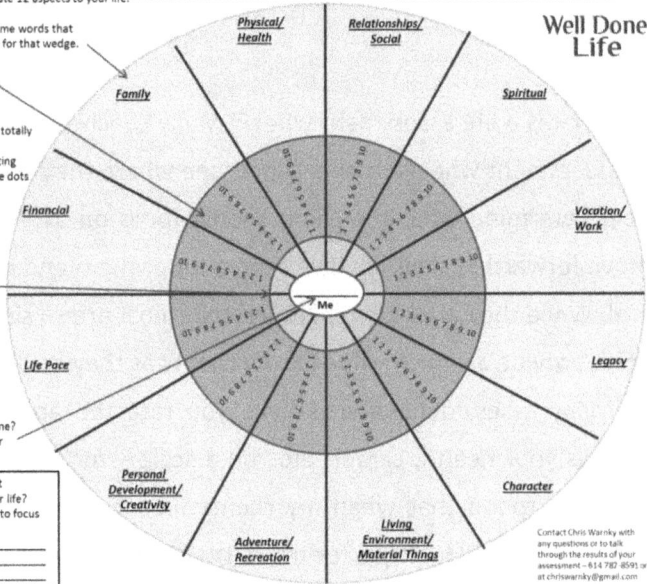

Instructions
In this exercise you will evaluate 12 aspects to your life.

Your Personal Life Assessment Wheel

Well Done Life

1. In the outer circle, write some words that describe your ideal or dream for that wedge.

2. In the dark blue circle, rate where you are today relative to living out your dream level for each wedge, with 10 representing you are totally living your dream now. Put a dot in the wedge reflecting Your rating. Then connect the dots across the circle to reflect a wheel.

3. Next, in the inner circle, Identify your ideal world top 4 categories with an "A" and then define your next 4 most important areas with a "B". Then, rank the A's and B's 1 through 4 (1 being most important) to reflect how important each of these areas are to you.

4. What one word describes who you want to be or become? Place that word on the center of the wheel.

Through this exercise, what sticks out to you about your life? What areas would you like to focus on at this time?
1. _____
2. _____
3. _____

Physical/ Health — Relationships/ Social — Family — Spiritual — Financial — Vocation/ Work — Me — Life Pace — Legacy — Personal Development/ Creativity — Character — Adventure/ Recreation — Living Environment/ Material Things

Contact Chris Warnky with any questions or to talk through the results of your assessment – 614 787-8591 or at chriswarnky@gmail.com

The Process

Once a client has defined their top rating and rated themselves in each segment of the wheel, I have them use the next inner circle to identify the categories that are the most important to them. First they identify their top four priorities, placing an "A" in each of those wedges, then they place a "B" in the wedges of the next four most important categories. Then I ask them to rank the four "A" categories, 1 through 4, making the hard decisions about the priority of each category.

The next step is for them to define a word (or a couple of words) that best reflect what they want their life to represent – a "life word" defining who they are or who they want to become. For me, that word is *steward*. I want to be an excellent faithful steward of all that God has provided. It's a powerful exercise to think this through and define your word.

Once my client has selected a word, they can use it to help guide their thoughts, decisions, actions, and investments – their days. It provides a target to aim for – guidance as they move through life, working to have everything they do fall in line with their life word.

The final step of the assessment-wheel process is to review what has been discovered from completing the wheel and then define the one to three categories the person feels are most important to focus on to move forward more intentionally with their life. My clients can then use various elements of the wheel to choose their priories. Some choose to focus on the categories with the lowest ratings. Some focus on the highest-priority A-rated categories regardless of how high their scores are in those categories. Others select an area of focus based on their "life word" in order to work on who they want to become.

After a wheel has been filled in and is providing needed focus, I recommend that it be reviewed and updated every six to 12 months. It should be reviewed as often as it feels helpful in providing holistic focus. It might be just once or several times – it's different for each person.

How to Use the Assessment Wheel

The assessment wheel can be used with a coach to help you intentionally focus on moving forward with your life. You can use it yourself for that purpose or as structure for a Refocus Session. And it can be used to communicate your efforts to those close to you. The completed form truly reflects your current place in life and the heartfelt desire you have to become who you want to be in the future.

I've both shared and used the Well Done Life – Life Assessment Wheel with clients, and I've also shared it with friends and acquaintances I thought would gain value from it. When they've felt overwhelmed and stuck, the structure and the simple process have been helpful for them. And I've personally gained tremendous clarity by using this assessment wheel.

One client so appreciated this wheel that in addition to using it in our coaching sessions she shared it with her husband and children. She felt it was an excellent way to share where she was in her life and how she wanted to move forward. Her kids in particular loved it and asked if they could also complete one so they could better share their lives with their mom. I encouraged her to give them the form and she reported that it was a fantastic way to share deeply about where she was and where they were in their lives.

The form is copyrighted by Well Done Life, LLC, but may be shared for the benefit of you and others. I do ask that you not use it in a professional capacity without permission.

Chapter 14

Other Context-Providing Assessments

After Experiences

I find significant value in completing targeted assessments after major events I've prepared for and performed. This includes speeches I give, meetings I lead, books I write, ninja competitions I compete in, and new ninja skills I try.

I leave the venue and stop at a park or visit a restaurant and order a fountain drink. For about 30 minutes I sit and think about the experience to see what I can learn to help me improve and grow. The "went well" elements are very satisfying and worth appreciating and celebrating. The "not so well" can provide encouragement, especially when I realize that there are simple things I can do better to make a big difference in how I will perform and the results I will deliver in the future. Then I develop a "next steps" plan outlining what to focus on or change for the next time I'm in a similar situation.

This is a simple way to grow and build on your experiences. The information is fresh in your mind if you pause right after a major event or activity to assess and improve for the future, and you're less likely to forget something important to your assessment. Give this a try, and make a habit of planning for this time along with your plans for such activities.

Tracking Lessons Learned

I make notes throughout my writing process. Once a book is fully published, I compile my notes and add them to an Excel document I call "Lessons Learned" so I can refer to them and apply them to future books. I've learned a great deal about writing and publishing, and I've made notes about the writing experience, my manuscript review process, the feedback from beta readers, and especially regarding the revisions recommended by my professional editor. I hope over time she has seen improvement in the manuscripts she has received from me.

Many don't prioritize taking time to ensure that they learn from key experiences, but when you think in this way you can learn from anything and everything. It's one more way to make your life rich and more valuable for yourself and others. This is really a quick and simple process. I've made countless, often simple improvements in how I prepare for and deliver my engagements. With a little intention, you too can gain these same benefits.

Chapter 15

Easy Love Matrix

Years ago, as a corporate manager, I developed a simple assessment tool to help me and my staff better align ourselves with the work we had to do. I had read books about the value of aligning your work with what is naturally easy for you to do and what you love or have a passion for. This led me to create a simple matrix. The name I gave it was the Easy to Do/Love to Do Matrix. The short version is the Easy Love Matrix, or ELM. The name brought a grin to people's faces.

This tool helped my staff segment their work assignments into the various matrix attributes. Then I met with each of them to talk about finding ways to do more of what was easy for them and that they loved to do. With things that were particularly hard for someone, or that they hated to do, we talked about ways to reassign that work to others who were a better fit or we looked for tools or additional training that could make the work less taxing for them. In some cases we talked about the possibility of the person moving into a completely different role that was a better fit for them. Because there were several people on our team, we were able to move a number of tasks to people who were a better fit, resulting in better performances and happier, more engaged employees who enjoyed their jobs more.

Here is the matrix:

Easy-to-do/Love-to-do Matrix

Instructions: Add to each block, all significant current and past activities you have done.
* Current Work Activities   * Current Personal Activities (optional)
* Past Work Activities   * Past Personal Activities (optional)

Strategy		Love to Do - Energizing *Find Ways To Do More of This*	Prefer Not to Do - Somewhat Draining	Really Don't Like to Do - Very Draining *Find Other Ways to Get This Done*	
	Very Easy to Do	Organize things and events Prioritize: goals, tasks, etc. Think about the future and possibilities Format documents for presentations Create documents Plan things Analyze numerical data and Facilitate group meetings Coach people on life management			
	Takes Significant Effort	Read management concept books	Write status reports	Read detailed emails Approach senior management with Work through a backlog of emails	
					Strategy
	Very Hard to Do - Very Draining		Make formal verbal presentations Listen to long detailed conference	Generate detailed meeting minutes Put in call to resolve service issues Complete customer service request Represent business	

You start in the second column, which is the "happy" column — the "Love to Do – Energizing" column. This is where I hoped the majority of a person's tasks would be listed. The middle column is for tasks you would "Prefer Not to Do – Somewhat Draining." The next column is for the "Really Don't Like to Do – Very Draining" tasks. The goal is to have little in this column. That wasn't always the case when my staff filled out the matrix.

The sections under those column headings further divide the tasks into three categories. The top section is for listing "Very Easy to Do" tasks; the middle section is for "Takes Significant Effort," and the bottom section is for tasks that are "Very Hard to Do – Very Draining"; these are the types of things that make you hate your job, dread going to work, and want to quit. The goal was to have little, if anything, in that line.

The "Strategy" boxes are for listing actions you can take to leverage your particular personality traits and preferences. To take
advantage of my strengths, mine would include actions like using my
organizational experience to define a rotation order for teaching obstacle skills at MLab Ohio, or creating a template for communicating
with my coaching clients. Or, to limit actions that I don't do as well, I
might record a reminder to ask someone else to document details at
a meeting or follow up on resolving an equipment or systems issue.

Some of your assignments require you to do things that are hard
and that you don't like to do, but if these tasks comprise the majority
of your job, you're poorly matched to your work. It would take tremendous intention to grow in that type of role. Such a situation can
result in a poor attitude, an unhappy work life in which you're just
working to make ends meet, and possibly an unhappy life in general
in which the primary focus is just getting by. If you don't work toward
changing your situation, you might never progress to a better fit for
yourself.

A few examples from my completed form include the following
from my "Love to Do/Very Easy to Do" box: "Organize things and
events," "Prioritize goals and tasks," and "Think about the future and
possibilities." In my "Really Don't Like to Do/Very Hard to Do" box I
listed things like "Generate detailed content," "Generate meeting
minutes," and "Present complex business details and processes."

I also used this matrix to convey to my boss who I am and what I
loved to do and did well. As a result we were able to modify some of
my tasks, giving me more opportunities to work on developmental
activities for the whole staff, not just my staff. I was able to limit the
amount of detailed business processes I needed to understand and

do presentations regarding in front of large groups. We were able to identify others who were better suited for those aspects of the job. Taking the time to work through this exercise also sent a strong message that I cared about my staff and wanted to help them succeed.

You can use this matrix to determine how well you fit your current work role and other commitments you've made outside of your workplace. It allows you to quickly summarize your world and how well your current commitments fit who you are. I hope you find it beneficial for some aspect of your life.

Chapter 16

Planning and Energy Management

For a long time I felt that learning to manage my time would be the real game-changer for my productivity. In a sense it was. In attempting to manage my time I was much more intentional about planning and scheduling, and my productivity seemed to skyrocket. But we all have the same amount of time, so we don't really manage time; we manage how we use it, – how we prioritize our 24 hours of each day. This is a valuable focus, and those who strive to use their time intentionally are usually much more productive than those who don't.

I don't mean to take away from the value I gained from my time-management efforts, but now I believe it's even more important to focus on managing my *energy*, which is the most important subset of my time. While we all have the same amount of time, we don't have the same amount of energy. And even if we did, we don't all leverage our energy in the same ways. All minutes aren't created equal. Some include high energy, drive, and motivation, and some feel like we're wasting or killing time. My goal is to do what I can to generate high-energy, motivational minutes, knowing that having even three to five hours of high energy in a day is much more powerful than living unintentionally, hoping that every once in a while I'll feel energized.

Matching Volume to Capacity

I love the concept of matching volume to capacity. I've experienced the importance of identifying my capacity – how much time and energy I have available for an hour, a day, a week, or maybe even month – and then planning to accomplish only the most important things with my available time until I've used all my projected capacity.

If you're like me, there are things on your mind that you feel you need to do, must do, should do, and want to do. Getting everything on your list done often takes more time than you have.

You have only a certain number of discretionary hours available each day, and many of your responsibilities aren't negotiable: sleeping, eating, showers, classes, meetings, dropping off or picking up the kids – you name it. These come first. It's the balance of your day that defines your true discretionary capacity.

There have been many days when I hadn't planned to do specific things on my to-do list or hadn't defined how many of them I could get done. When that to-do list is very long and I'm not intentional, it can feel overwhelming, and I jump in haphazardly doing things in order to get at least a little of it done that day. It feels depressing as I trudge through the day, barely making a dent in my mountain of to-dos. Even what I do get done can feel insignificant, with little impact on the whole. Both during the day and at the end of the day, it felt disheartening. Even when I work hard and do a lot, it sometimes doesn't translate into achievement because I did not have the needed structure in place.

I've learned a totally new way to approach my workday. It has changed my world and my feelings about my days. Busy days can now be enjoyable and satisfying, even when at the end of the day there's still much that needed to be done that didn't get done. When I match, or limit my volume of work to my true available capacity, I come away energized, knowing I did all I could do – all I had the ability to do – for that time period. It's a wonderful feeling at the end of the hour or day.

Each day I define how much time I have to work on my to-do list. Then I identify what's most important, project an amount of time it will take me to complete those top items, and cull the list to fit the time I have available – there's no reason to feel the pressure of getting those things done when I don't have the time to begin with. Then I focus on and get the items I chose done. Some days I get all of my list done and I even have time to do one or two more. It's a fantastic feeling when I get to do that. Some days I underestimate how much time it will take to get something done, and I don't quite complete my list. Even in these cases I only feel bad about the one or two items I didn't accomplish, not the whole mountain that was previously on my mind.

Give this method a try. It can literally change your day and life. It's simple and powerful – just a change of perspective.

Energy Management Assessment

To help me focus on my energy, I created a simple "Energy Management Assessment":

Energy Management Assessment

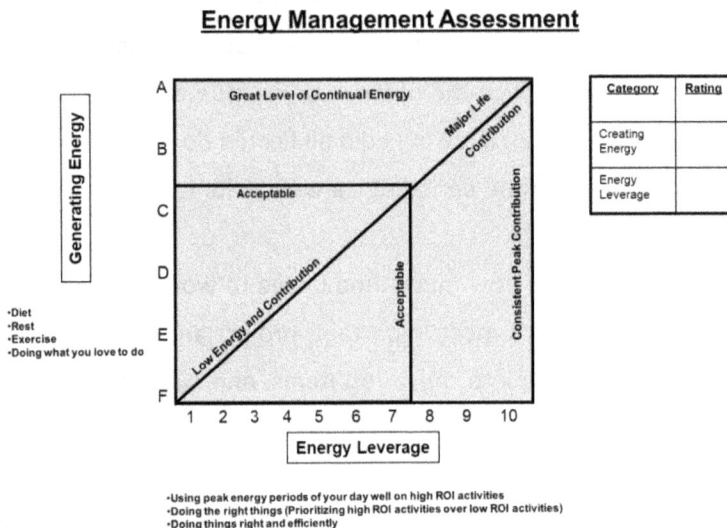

The vertical axis reflects how well I generate energy, which I believe I can definitely impact; and the horizontal axis reflects how well I *use* my energy.

I see the "Generating Energy" elements as how well I'm managing my diet, rest, exercise, and the things I love to do. When I do these things, I find that I generate more energy. When I'm weak in any one of these, it spills into other areas and I feel drained and unmotivated – clearly not energized. It makes sense to do what I can to maximize my energy.

The "Energy Leverage" axis reflects how well I'm using the peak energy periods of my day – how well I'm leveraging my high return-on-investment (ROI) activities. Am I doing the right things – prioritizing the most important things versus doing something urgent that's in front of me? Am I doing things right? Am I doing things efficiently? These are the three criteria for evaluating how well I'm leveraging my energy.

The goal is to be as close as I can to an A10 score, where I'm making a major life contribution. You might find this assessment helpful as you work to maximize your energy.

Planning Assessment

I also developed an assessment tool to look at how well I've planned my time and actions. How intentional have I been versus just letting each day happen?

I believe we should live in the moment, enjoying and maximizing how we use each minute of the day. However, I also believe we should invest quality time in planning ahead. Planning ahead is a tremendous practice for generating better results. Intentionally planning helps me make better moment-by-moment decisions because I know where I want to go and I know what it will take to get there. Each momentary decision then has clarity, purpose, and direction, and it's easier to make decisions that benefit me and provide the results I want for my life, family, friends, and business.

The "Planning Window Assessment" below is a simple way to evaluate how far out I'm planning. I'm aware that there are those who continually look five, 10, or more years ahead, but I feel like I'm being intentional if I'm generally looking one year ahead. There are of course certain aspects of life that require planning further ahead. For example, 20 years prior to reaching 57, I planned to retire at that age; my financial plan extends 50 years into the future; and my book-writing plan includes a 10-year look forward. But when I need a quick overview I use this window to assess how I'm approaching life.

The scale is from 0 to 8; 0 being just doing without planning, and 8 representing a longer-than-one-year plan.

Planning Window Assessment

How do you rate yourself based on the scale in the chart below? Determine how far out are you planning the activities of your life, and the corresponding number is your rate. Use that number to inspire yourself to think longer-term. I am happy to report that I'm currently giving myself an 8.

Planning Window	Scale
Not planning, just doing	0
The next hour	1
Today	2
Through the next day	3
The upcoming week	4
The upcoming month	5
The upcoming quarter	6
The upcoming year	7
Longer than one year	8

What do you believe about planning? Where are you today on this scale? If you have questions or would like more information about any of these tools you can reach out to me at chriswarn-ky@gmail.com.

Chapter 17

Getting Support

Sometimes you invest a significant amount of time and a good deal of effort, but you still aren't able to accomplish something or become the person you want to become. When you're in this situation, often the best action is to seek some outside help.

Having an accountability partner is powerful and can help you achieve that goal. Sometimes, however, even that is not enough. You need to seek yet additional support.

Support can come in various forms. Sometimes you need to learn something to move forward. That can come from reading a book, watching a video, or learning from an expert. Other times you need to participate in a program in which you gain expertise from someone else so you don't have to learn it the hard way.

Learning about my Refocus Sessions from this book is a form of getting coaching – self-coaching. Coaching is extremely powerful when done well. That's why I took the time to write and publish *Refocus*. But sometimes it's difficult to follow such a process by yourself, and your results might not be as comprehensive as you would like them to be. This is when it's reasonable to consider hiring a professional coach.

A well-trained professional coach, partnering side-by-side with you to lead you through assessment processes like those in this book, can be extremely helpful because they bring an objective viewpoint to the process. I provided you with structure for your refocusing efforts, but a coach can help you work through that structure.

Sometimes the level of self-discipline required to work through a process on your own can be overwhelming and challenging. A coach might push you to think harder about your answer to a question than you would on your own. They can help you get much clearer about your responses, as it's easy to respond too generally to assessment questions. The more tangible your responses, the greater the value.

It's also easy to get impatient with yourself and to want to move on to the next step when you feel stuck. A coach is supportive, patient, and helps you go much deeper into the experience. They can help you better understand the "whys" behind your thoughts, hopes, and dreams, and they can help you gain more clarity by asking deep questions.

If you're like most of us, it's easy to get down on yourself, especially when your life isn't what you want it to be. A coach is a partner who helps you accept where you are without judgment, and focuses you forward on what you want and how you can get there.

Finally, having a coach also forces you to block out the time to think. This is one of the hardest parts. You can create a plan and then have the daily responsibilities of life repeatedly preempt your plan so that you never really get around to taking the dedicated, quality, focused time you know you need and want.

You can do much on your own, especially if you're a disciplined person, but having a coach provides benefits and value that you won't get on your own. If you want to receive the value of Refocus Sessions and you can't seem to get there on your own, you might want to try hiring a coach.

Conclusion

It's easy to slip into a "go with the flow" mindset and not live intentionally, missing what's going on in the big picture of your life. When you take the time to stop, observe, and think about where you are, what's going on, and where you want to go, you will change and improve your life, which will also positively impact the lives of your loved ones and others.

I hope you see how important it is to take the time to refocus your life. I hope my experience as reflected in this book is a useful model and an encouragement to you, that one of the Refocus Session levels works well for you, and that one or more of the additional assessment tools I shared is helpful as you invest more time and effort in assessing how you're living your life and how you could potentially live even better, making an even bigger impact on your family and on the world.

I'm convinced that using these tools and processes can help you become even more confident and intentional about your life. They have been powerful for me and I'm sure they can be for you as well.

I'm excited for you. You've invested in yourself by reading *Refocus*. It will pay off. You and your family will have a better future because you've invested time in who you're becoming.

Make it another great day, week, month, and year.
Chris Warnky

Refocus Session Forms

Five Feet Deep Level

Be Present (10–30 minutes)

Clear your mind and focus on your new surroundings.

Pluses and Minuses

+ (What's going well?)	− (What's not going as well?)	Possible actions

+ (What's going well?)	− (What's not going as well?)	Possible actions

Application

List 2–4 actions from above to plan for.

Twenty Feet Deep Level

Be Present (10–30 minutes)

Clear your mind and focus on your new surroundings

Thanks Time

Key Life Areas

Life Area	What's going well?	What's not going well?	Actions to Take

Life Area	What's going well?	What's not going well?	Actions to Take

Three Questions

What should I be focusing on that I'm not? _____

_____

_____

What decision or decisions do I need to be making that I'm delaying?

_____

_____

_____

What do I need to say no to? _____

_____

Application

List 2–4 actions from above to plan for.

_____

_____

_____

_____

_____

Fifty Feet Deep Level

Be Present (10–30 minutes)

Clear your mind and focus on your new surroundings.

Thanks Time

How is God currently working in my life beyond the many basics He provides daily?

Key Life Areas

Life Area	+ (What's going well?)	− (What's not going as well?)	Possible actions

Key Life Areas (cont.) (Copy this page to record more.)

Life Area	What's going well?	What's not going as well?	Possible actions

Three Questions

What should I be focusing on that I'm not?

_____

_____

_____

_____

_____

What decision or decisions do I need to be making that I'm delaying?

_____

_____

_____

_____

_____

What do I need to say no to?

_____

_____

_____

_____

_____

Word Picture

_____

_____

_____

_____

_____

_____

_____

Coach Yourself

Identify an earlier topic that lends itself to the coaching process:

_____

Define what you want in regard to this topic.

_____

_____

_____

What have you tried to get those results?

_____

_____

_____

_____

_____

How has that worked?

_____

_____

_____

_____

_____

Identify more options for improvement:

_____

_____

_____

_____

_____

Select actions for moving forward:

_____

_____

_____

_____

_____

Annual Goals

Goal	Progress/Actions

Evaluate One Governing Value

_____

_____

_____

_____

_____

Journal Review

_____

_____

_____

_____

_____

Look 10 Years Out

_____

_____

_____

_____

_____

_____

_____

Application Matrix

Stop doing	Start doing
Do less	Do more

Learn More

Contact Information

Chris Warnky, author, ninja competitor, executive and life coach, motivational speaker, trainer, and owner of Well Done Life, LLC

Cell phone: 614.787.8591

Email: chriswarnky@gmail.com

Facebook: welldonelife

Website: welldone-life.com

Blog: http://cwarnky.wordpress.com

Be Coached by Chris

Chris provides both executive and life coaching, in person and virtually.

Want Chris to Speak to Your Group?

Chris is available to speak to groups on a variety of topics including:

- His *Well Done Life* and *Heart of a Ninja* series books
- Personal refocus retreats
- Leadership and communication topics
- John Maxwell Team leadership materials

Thirteen percent of initial profits from sales of Chris's books are donated to charitable organizations.

Acknowledgments

I'm thankful to our awesome Creator/God for allowing me to live 64 years and for providing me with countless relationships and experiences. I'm also thankful to have peace with Him because of the life and sacrifice of His Son, Jesus.

Thanks to my wife, Carolyn, for your love, and especially for your support while I've been writing, editing, and publishing this and other books. I can't imagine going through life without you by my side to celebrate our successes and to support each other in times of failure and disappointment. I love you!

Thanks to those who have shared that they are intrigued by this topic and my journey and who have asked me to share my processes.

There are countless others I'm thankful to for their contributions to my life and for their help with writing, editing, and feedback on *Refocus*. Just a few of them include Mom and Dad — thanks for the love and support you've provided throughout my life. Thank you, Tim, Bonnie, Michelle, and Joel, for your love and support. Thanks also to Shanon Paglieri for your continual friendship, support, and encouragement, especially with my books; thanks again for reading and providing valuable feedback as my beta reader of *Refocus*. And thanks to Gwen Hoffnagle, my professional editor for all of my first seven books. You continue to take my original manuscripts to new and much higher levels. I enjoy working with you and appreciate the value you provide. Thank you so much!

About the Author

Chris Warnky is 64 years young, and has been married to Carolyn May Warnky for over 41 years. He has two children. His son, Tim, lives in Cleveland with his wife, Bonnie, and two daughters. His daughter, Michelle Warnky-Buurma, lives in Willard, Ohio, with her husband Joel. She is a popular multiyear *American Ninja Warrior* competitor and a competitive obstacle-course racer.

Chris is an active ninja warrior who competed in the 2017 *ANW Cleveland City Qualifier.* He's also an MLAB OH staff member and Ninja Lite instructor. He provides personal one-on-one ninja-lite-level targeted training sessions.

Chris has been a Bible-reading Christian for over 50 years. His relationship with God is the basis for his life.

He's the author of seven books with plans to write several more, a professional executive and life coach, and a thought-provoking speak-  er through his business, Well Done Life. He coaches clients in addressing important life and business topics.

Chris is a certified coach, speaker, and trainer with the John Maxwell Team. He served two years on the organization's President's Advisory Council. He served two terms as the International Coach Federation Columbus Charter

Chapter president. He achieved the Toastmasters International "Competent Communicator" designation.

Chris has over three decades of corporate leadership experience, including 23 years as a vice president at Bank One/JP Morgan Chase contributing as a compensation manager, project manager, and program manager.

www.ingramcontent.com/pod-product-compliance
Lightning Source LLC
Chambersburg PA
CBHW071533040426
42452CB00008B/1004